The 4 ingredient Cookbook

As easy as 1,2,3,4

Cover designer: Sam Grimmer
Food Editor: Ellen Argyriou
Typesetting: Palmer Higgs, Box Hill, VIC Australia

The 4 Ingredient Cookbook
Published in 2003 by Hinkler Books Pty Ltd
17–23 Redwood Drive
Dingley VIC 3172 Australia
www.hinklerbooks.com

Previously published as The Ultimate Cooking with 4 Ingredients by Cookbook Resources, Texas, USA in 2002

Reprinted 2004

ISBN 1 8651 5698 1
Printed and bound in China

Introduction

In our fast-paced, rush-here-and-there lives, a home-cooked meal may be considered a luxury. We live out of our cars, placing food orders on mobile phones and going to drive-through windows for the night's meal and maybe the family sits down together to eat.

We hope to help families come back to the table and spend quality time while sharing good food to eat. The recipes in *The 4 Ingredient Cookbook* are easy to prepare and the ingredients are readily available. Most of them are already in your pantry.

Everyone in the family can cook out of *The 4 Ingredient Cookbook*. Mouth-watering meals are just minutes away and every minute we spend around the table enriches our lives and helps us grow stronger. Have a good time with this cookbook and don't hesitate to recruit some helpers.

It's a great time for all of us to come back to the table.

Jean C. Coates

Contents

APPETISERS and BEVERAGES

Chorizo Cheese Dip

340 g pork chorizo, sliced

1 (250 g) jar cheddar cheese spread

1 (400 g) can diced tomatoes

Tortillas

- Saute chorizo until cooked; drain. In a double boiler, melt the cheese spread and tomatoes.
- Combine chorizo and cheese mixture, blending well. Add a $^{1}/_{4}$ teaspoon chilli powder if desired. Serve with tortilla chips.

Speedy Cheese Dip

1 (35 g) packet cheese sauce mix

1 (400 g) can diced tomatoes and onion

1 (300 g) can cream chicken soup

Pinch of cayenne pepper

- Prepare the cheese sauce to packet directions.
- Stir in the remaining ingredients and heat through. Serve hot with potato crisps.

Spicy Beef and Cheese Dip

$^{3}/_{4}$ (of a 425 g can) diced tomatoes with black pepper and garlic

$^{1}/_{2}$ teaspoon chilli powder

1 (1 kg) box processed cheddar cheese, cubed

450 g lean minced beef, browned until crumbly and moisture absorbed

- In a large saucepan, place tomatoes, pepper and garlic, chilli powder and cheese.
- Heat on low until cheese melts. Add the ground beef, mixing well.
- Serve with tortilla chips.

Egg and Cheese Dip

5 hardcooked eggs, mashed

1 cup mayonnaise

120 g shredded tasty cheddar cheese

$^1/_2$ teaspoon prepared mustard

- In bowl, combine all ingredients and mix well. Add salt to taste. Refrigerate. Serve with wheat crackers.

Velvet Dip

1 (1 kg) box processed cheddar cheese, cubed

2 cups mayonnaise

1 (115 g) jar chopped pimentos (red pepper)

1 (250 g) jar jalapeno chilli slices, drained and chopped

- Place cheese in saucepan and melt over low heat.
- Add other ingredients and mix well. Serve with potato crisps.

Veggie Dip

1 (600 ml carton) sour cream

1 (250 g) packet frozen, chopped spinach, thawed, well drained

1 packet dry vegetable soup mix

1 bunch fresh green onions (shallots), chopped with tops

- Combine all ingredients (make sure spinach is well drained).
- Chill for several hours before serving (adding $^3/_4$ cup chopped pecans would be good in this dip). Serve with crackers.

Creamy Onion Dip

1 (500 g) packet cream cheese, softened

3 tablespoons lemon juice

1 packet dry onion soup mix

1 (300 mL) carton sour cream

- Beat cream cheese until smooth. Blend in lemon juice and onion soup mix.
- Gradually fold in sour cream until well blended.
- Chill. Serve with potato crisps, crackers or fresh vegetables.

Cold Curry Dip

$1^1/_2$ cups mayonnaise

2 teaspoons curry powder

1 tablespoon grated onion

$^1/_2$ teaspoon dry mustard

- Combine mayonnaise, curry powder, onion and mustard.
- Chill at least 1 hour before serving. Several dashes of Tabasco may be added.

Serve with chilled vegetables such as celery sticks, sliced zucchini or carrot sticks.

Fiesta Onion Dip

1 packet dry onion soup mix

1 (425 g) can diced tomatoes with garlic and black pepper

2 teaspoons chilli powder

1 cup grated cheddar cheese

- In small saucepan heat soup mix, tomatoes and chilli powder. Bring to the boil.
- Turn heat down and simmer for 20 minutes, stirring occasionally.
- To serve, pour into a serving bowl and sprinkle with the cheese. Stir before serving. Serve with potato crisps or corn chips.

Broccoli Cheese Dip

1 (35 g) packet cheese sauce mix, prepared to packet directions

$^1/_2$ (500 g) packet frozen broccoli, thawed and chopped

$^1/_2$ cup sour cream, $^1/_2$ teaspoon seasoned salt

2 teaspoons Dijon style mustard

- In a saucepan combine sauce, broccoli, sour cream, salt and mustard, mixing well. Heat and serve hot. Serve with corn ships.

Hot Broccoli Dip

1 (1 kg) box processed cheddar cheese, diced

1 (415 g) can cream of mushroom soup

1 (500 g) box frozen broccoli, thawed and chopped

Corn chips

- In saucepan, melt cheese with the soup and stir in broccoli. Heat thoroughly. Serve hot with corn chips.

Broccoli Dip

$^1/_2$ (500 g) packet frozen broccoli, thawed and chopped

1 (415 g) can cream of chicken soup

3 cups grated cheddar cheese

1 (250 g) jar jalapeno chilli drained and chopped

- In a saucepan, cook broccoli about 5 minutes in a little margarine and about $^1/_2$ teaspoon salt.
- Add soup, cheese and jalapeno.
- Heat until cheese melts. Serve with tostados.

Artichoke–Blue Cheese Dip

150 g butter

1 (400 g) can artichoke hearts, drained, chopped

150 g blue cheese

2 teaspoons lemon juice

- In a frying pan, melt butter and mix in artichoke hearts.
- Add blue cheese and lemon juice. Serve hot with crackers.

Artichoke–Bacon Dip

1 (340 g) jar marinated artichoke hearts, drained, chopped

1 cup mayonnaise

2 teaspoons worcestershire sauce

5 slices bacon, cooked crisp, crumbled

- In large bowl, combine all ingredients.
- Pour into a buttered 20 cm baking dish.
- Bake at 180°C for 12 minutes.
- Serve hot with crackers.

Sassy Onion Dip

1 (250 g) packet cream cheese, softened

1 (300 mL) carton sour cream

½ cup chilli sauce

1 packet dry onion soup mix

- Beat cream cheese until fluffy.
- Add remaining ingredients and mix well.
- Cover and chill.
- Serve with strips of raw zucchini, celery, carrots, etc.

Cottage Dip

1 (500 g) tub cottage cheese

1 envelope dry onion soup mix

$^1/_2$ cup mayonnaise

$^1/_2$ teaspoon garlic powder

- Blend all ingredients.
- Chill and serve with chips, crackers or vegetable sticks.

Hot-to-Trot Dip

500 g minced beef

1 (1 kg) box processed cheddar cheese, cubed

$1^1/_2$ cups salsa

Several drops of Tabasco

- Brown ground beef and drain well.
- In saucepan, heat cheese and salsa until cheese is melted. Add Tabasco.
- Combine meat and cheese mixture. Serve hot with tortilla chips.

Five-Minute Dip

1 (250 g) packet cream cheese, softened

1 cup mayonnaise

1 packet dry salad dressing mix

$^1/_2$ onion, finely chopped

- Combine cream cheese and mayonnaise and beat until creamy.
- Stir in salad dressing mix and onion.
- Chill and serve with fresh vegetables.

Horsey Shrimp Dip

1 (200 g) can tiny prawns, chopped and drained

3 tablespoons cream-style horseradish

$^1/_3$ cup mayonnaise

$^1/_2$ teaspoon cajun seasoning

- Combine prawns, horseradish, mayonnaise and seasoning.
- Refrigerate. Serve with crackers.

Spinach–Artichoke Dip

2 (250 g) boxes frozen spinach, thawed, drained

1 (340 g) jar marinated artichoke hearts, drained, finely chopped

1 cup mayonnaise

2 cups shredded mozzarella cheese

- Drain spinach with several layers of paper towels.
- Combine spinach, artichoke hearts, mayonnaise and cheese and mix well.
- Cover and refrigerate. Serve with corn chips or potato crisps.

Sombrero Dip

1 (400 g) can savoury mince

1 teaspoon Mexican style chilli powder

$^3/_4$ cup green chilli sauce

1 tablespoon chopped black olives

- Combine savoury mince and chilli powder in saucepan. Warm over low heat.
- Stir in sauce and olives. Serve with corn chips.

Avocado Ole!

3 large ripe avocados, mashed

1 tablespoon fresh lemon juice

1 packet dry onion soup mix

1 (300 mL) carton sour cream

- Mix avocados with lemon juice and blend in soup mix and sour cream. You may want to add a little salt. Serve with potato crisps or crackers.

Talking Tomato Dip

$^{2}/_{3}$ (425 g) can diced tomatoes with garlic and black pepper

1 (300 ml) carton sour cream

$1^{1}/_{2}$ teaspoons seasoned salt

2 teaspoons horseradish cream

- Combine all ingredients. Chill. Serve with crisps or crackers.

Watercress 'To Do' Dip

3 ripe avocados

$1^{1}/_{4}$ cups finely chopped watercress

$^{3}/_{4}$ cup mayonnaise

$^{1}/_{4}$ teaspoon ground cumin seeds

- Peel and mash softened avocados and place in medium bowl.
- Add the watercress, mayonnaise and cumin seeds and mix well.
- Add salt to taste.
- Cover and refrigerate. Serve with potato crisps.

Picante Cream

1 (300 mL) carton sour cream

$^1/_2$ teaspoon prepared mustard

$^1/_2$ cup hot picante sauce

$^1/_2$ teaspoon celery salt

- Combine all ingredients.
- Chill. Serve with potato crisps or crackers.

Whiz Bang Dip

700 g minced beef

$^1/_4$ cup chopped onion

1 (1 kg) box processed cheddar cheese, cubed

$^3/_4$ cup Thousand Island dressing

- In saucepan brown meat and onion on high heat until juice is absorbed.
- Reduce heat to low and combine all ingredients, mixing well.
- Cook until cheese is melted, stirring constantly. Serve with potato crisps or corn chips.

Pep-Pep-Pepperoni Dip

2 (250 g) packets cream cheese, softened

100 g pepperoni slices

1 (340 mL) bottle chilli sauce

1 bunch fresh green onions with tops, chopped

- In mixing bowl, beat cream cheese until creamy.
- Cut pepperoni slices into smaller chunks.
- Add pepperoni, chilli sauce and green onions to the cream cheese and mix well.
- Refrigerate. Serve with potato chips.

Dried Beef and Chips

1 (250 g) packet cream cheese, softened

1 (300 mL) carton sour cream

2 (50 g) packets dried beef (biltong), chopped

$^1/_2$ cup finely chopped pecans

- In mixing bowl, combine cream cheese and sour cream and beat until creamy.
- Fold in dried beef and pecans.
- Refrigerate. Serve with chips.

Whip-It-Up Dip

2 (50 g) packets dried beef (biltong), coarsely chopped

1 (250 g) packet shredded cheddar cheese

$^2/_3$ cup mayonnaise

$^2/_3$ teaspoon garlic powder

- Combine all ingredients and mix well. (The easiest way to chop dried beef is with scissors.) Serve with crackers.

If you would rather serve it hot, you may spread the mixture on crackers and bake at 180°C for about 8 minutes.

Confetti Dip

1 (420 g) can whole kernel corn, drained

1 (420 g) can black beans, drained

$^1/_3$ cup Italian salad dressing

1 (375 g) jar salsa

- Combine all ingredients together.
- Refrigerate several hours before serving. Serve with crackers.

Fun Mustard Dip

1 cup white vinegar

1 (55 g) can dry mustard

3 eggs, well beaten

1 cup sugar

- Combine vinegar and mustard and mix well. Refrigerate 24 hours.
- Add eggs and sugar and mix well. Cook on low, stirring until thickened.
- Pour into jars and refrigerate. Serve with cocktail sausages or any food served with mustard.

Ham-Bone Dip

1 (500 g) packet cream cheese, softened

2 (170 g) cans devilled ham

1 heaped tablespoon prepared horseradish

1/4 cup finely chopped onion

- In mixer, beat cream cheese until creamy.
- Add all other ingredients. Chill and serve with crackers.

Pepper-Pot Bean Dip

1 (430 g) can refried beans

1 (500 g) box processed cheddar cheese, cubed

120 g margarine

1 teaspoon garlic powder or Mexican-style chilli powder, to taste

- In a large double boiler, combine all ingredients.
- Heat on low, stirring often, until cheese and margarine melt.
- Serve hot in a chafing dish (candleburner). Serve with tortilla chips.

Crunchy Asparagus Dip

1 (340 g) can asparagus spears, drained, chopped

1/2 cup mayonnaise

1/4 teaspoon Tabasco

1/2 cup chopped pecans

- Combine all ingredients in a medium bowl.
- Refrigerate.
- Serve with wheat thins or crackers.

Party Shrimp Dip

1 (250 g) packet cream cheese, softened

1/2 cup mayonnaise

1 (200 g) can tiny, cooked prawns, drained

3/4 teaspoon creole seasoning or Mexican-style chilli powder

- Blend cream cheese and mayonnaise in mixer. Stir in prawns and seasoning.
- Mix well and chill. Serve with crackers.

Quickie Prawn Dunk

1 (250 g) packet cream cheese, softened

1 (250 g) bottle cocktail sauce

1 teaspoon Italian seasoning

1 (200 g) can tiny prawns, drained

- Place cream cheese in mixing bowl and beat until it is smooth.
- Add remaining ingredients and chill. Serve with crackers.

Chunky Prawn Dip

2 (200 g) cans prawns, drained

2 cups mayonnaise

6 green onions, finely chopped

$^3/_4$ cup chunky salsa

- Crumble prawns and stir in mayonnaise, onion and salsa.
- Chill for 1 to 2 hours. Serve with crackers.

Tasty Tuna Dip

1 (200 g) can tuna in spring water, drained and flaked

1 teaspoon each garlic powder and dried oregano

1 (300 mL) carton sour cream

$^1/_4$ cup chopped black olives, drained

- Combine all ingredients, stirring until blended.
- Chill 8 hours. Serve with melba toast.

Cheesy-Crab Dip

1 (170 g) roll processed garlic cheese, diced

$^3/_4$ (of a 415 g) can cream of mushroom soup

1 (170 g) can crabmeat, drained

2 tablespoons sherry

- In medium-size pan heat all ingredients until cheese has melted.
- Keep warm in a chafing dish (candleburner) and serve with assorted crackers.

Gitty-Up Crab Dip

1 (250 g) packet cream cheese, softened

3 tablespoons salsa

2 tablespoons prepared horseradish

1 (170 g) can crabmeat, drained and flaked

- In mixing bowl, beat cream cheese until creamy.
- Add the salsa and horseradish and mix well.
- Stir in the crabmeat. Refrigerate. Serve with assorted crackers.

Hot, Rich Crab Dip

1 (35 g) cheese sauce mix, prepared to packet directions

1 (500 g) box processed cheddar cheese, cubed

2 (170 g) cans crabmeat, flaked

1 (500 g) jar salsa

- In a microwave bowl, combine the cheese sauce and cheddar cheese.
- Microwave at 1-minute intervals until cheese melts, stirring between intervals.
- Add the crabmeat and salsa, mixing well. Serve hot with corn chips.

Crab Crackers

1 (170 g) can crabmeat, drained and flaked

1 (250 g) packet cream cheese, softened

2 (295 g) cans cream of celery soup

2 tablespoons chopped black olives

- In a saucepan combine all ingredients until cheese melts. Serve hot with crackers.

You might also want to add several drops of Tabasco.

Unbelievable Crab Dip

1 (170 g) can white crabmeat, drained and flaked

1 (250 g) packet cream cheese

120 g butter

Chips or crackers

- In a saucepan combine crabmeat, cream cheese and butter.
- Heat and mix thoroughly. When mixed, transfer to chafing dish and serve with corn chips or crackers.

Easy Tuna Dip

1 (180 g) can tuna, drained

½ teaspoon each garlic powder and dried oregano

1 (300 mL) carton sour cream

2 green onions (shallots) with tops, chopped

- Combine all ingredients, mixing well. Let set several hours before serving.
- Salt, pepper to taste.
- Serve with crackers.

California Mussel Dip

1 envelope dry onion soup mix

1 (600 mL) carton sour cream

1 (250 g) tub mussels, drained, chopped

2 tablespoons chilli sauce

- Combine onion soup mix and sour cream and mix well. Add mussels and chilli sauce. Chill.

Velvet Mussel Dip

340 g cream cheese

50 g stick margarine

2 (100 g) cans smoked mussels, chopped

½ teaspoon worcestershire sauce

- Melt cream cheese and margarine in double boiler.
- Add chopped mussels and worcestershire sauce. Serve hot with crackers.

Cottage-Ham Dip

1 (500 g) carton cottage cheese, drained

3 (170 g) jars devilled ham

1 package dry onion soup mix

½ cup sour cream

- Blend cottage cheese in blender or with mixer.
- Add ham, soup mix and sour cream, mixing well. Serve with crackers.

Speedy Chilli Con Queso

1 (500 g) box processed cheddar cheese, cubed

½ cup milk

1 (340 g) jar salsa

Tortilla chips

- In saucepan, melt the cheese and milk in top of double boiler.
- Add about half the salsa. Serve with tortilla chips.

Taste and add more salsa as needed for desired heat!

Beef Roll

2 (250 g) packets cream cheese, softened

1/2 medium onion, grated

2 tablespoons lemon juice

1 (50 g) packet dried beef (biltong)

- Whip the cream cheese until fluffy. Season with grated onion, lemon juice and a couple of dashes of Tabasco.
- Place dried beef on a long roll of wax paper. Spread cream cheese thinly over the beef.
- Roll tightly and refrigerate. Cut into thin slices when ready to serve.

Sausage Balls

500 g hot pork sausage uncooked and skins removed

1 (500 g) packet grated cheddar cheese

3 cups scone mix

1/3 cup milk

- Combine all ingredients and form into small balls. If dough is a little too sticky, add a teaspoon more scone mix.
- Bake at 190°C for 13 to 15 minutes.

Hot Cheese Balls

1 (125 g) jar cheese spread

60 g margarine, softened

1/2 cup flour

1/8 teaspoon salt

- Mash cheese spread and the margarine, mixing well. Add flour and salt. Mix well.
- Roll into small balls. Chill one hour.
- Place on ungreased baking sheet.
- Bake at 210°C for 10 minutes. Balls will flatten as they cook. Serve hot.

Chilli-Cheese Balls

1 (225 g) packet grated sharp cheddar cheese, at room temperature

120 g stick margarine, softened

1 cup flour

1 teaspoon Mexican-style chilli powder

- Stir cheese and margarine together.
- Add flour, chilli powder and 1/2 teaspoon salt.
- Form dough into 5 cm (2 inch) balls and place on baking sheet. Bake at 190°C for 14 to 15 minutes.

Blue Cheese Ball

3 fresh green onions

1 (250 g) packet cream cheese, softened

1 (150 g) packet blue cheese, softened

1/3 cup chopped pecans

- Finely chop white portion of onions and combine with cream cheese and blue cheese, blending well. Shape into a ball.
- Finely chop green portion of onions and combine with pecans and roll cheese ball in the mixture to completely cover.
- Chill at least 3 hours. Serve on tooth picks.

Ranch Cheese Ball

1 packet dry ranch-style salad dressing mix

1 (500 g) packet cream cheese, softened

1/2 cup finely chopped pecans

85 g diced bacon, sauteed until crisp

- With mixer, stir together the dressing mix and cream cheese.
- Roll into a ball. Roll cheese ball in the pecans and bacon bits.
- Refrigerate several hours before serving.

Olive-Cheese Empanadas

1 cup pimento-stuffed green olives or black olives, chopped

1 cup finely shredded cheddar cheese

4 tablespoons mayonnaise

1 packet of 2 frozen short crust pastry sheets, thawed

- Preheat oven to 210°C. Combine the olives, cheese and mayonnaise.
- Using a $7^1/_2$-cm biscuit cutter, cut each pastry sheet into 12 rounds. Place 1 teaspoon of olive mixture in the centre of a pastry round. Lightly brush edge with water.
- Fold edge of pastry to the other side, press the edges together to seal.
- Crimp the edge with your thumb and forefinger or use the tines of a fork to seal the edges.
- Place on a baking tray and bake for about 10 minutes or until golden brown.

Spinach-Cheese Ball

1 (250 g) packet frozen chopped spinach, thawed

1 (500 g) packet cream cheese, softened

1 (35 g) packet dry vegetable soup mix

1 (225 g) can water chestnuts, chopped

- Drain spinach on paper towels. Squeeze or mash spinach into towels several times to make sure all water is gone from the spinach.
- In mixing bowl, beat the cream cheese until smooth. Fold in the spinach, soup mix and water chestnuts.
- Form into a ball and serve with crackers.

Beefy Cheese Balls

1 (500 g) packet cream cheese, softened

2 (50 g) packets dried beef (biltong)

1 bunch fresh green onions with tops, chopped

1 teaspoon cayenne pepper

- Beat cream cheese with mixer until smooth and creamy.
- Chop dried beef in food processor or blender.
- Combine the beef, cream cheese, onions and cayenne pepper.
- Form into a ball and chill overnight.

Serve with crackers.

Tuna Melt Appetiser

1 (250 g) packet frozen spinach, drained

2 (200 g) cans white tuna in water, drained, flaked

$^3/_4$ cup mayonnaise

$1^1/_2$ cups shredded mozzarella cheese, divided

- Drain spinach well with several paper towels.
- In a large bowl, combine spinach, tuna, mayonnaise and 1 cup cheese and mix well.
- Spoon into a buttered pie plate and bake at 180°C for 15 minutes. Remove from oven and sprinkle remaining cheese over top. Bake another 5 minutes. Serve with crackers.

Onion-Ham Dip

1 (125 g) jar cheddar cheese spread

1 (125 g) can devilled ham

1 cup mayonnaise

1 bunch fresh green onions (shallots), chopped

- In a medium bowl, combine cheese spread, ham and mayonnaise and mix until well blended.
- Fold in chopped green onions.

Serve with crackers.

Chicken-Cheese Spread

1 (500 g) packet cream cheese, softened

2 tablespoons worcestershire sauce

2 cups finely shredded, cooked chicken breasts

$^{1}/_{4}$ cup chopped almonds, toasted

- In mixer bowl, combine cream cheese and worcestershire sauce and beat until creamy.
- Fold in shredded chicken and almonds. Spread on English muffin halves and heat under moderate griller without browning.

English Muffin Pizza

English muffin, halved

Canned or bottled pizza sauce

Sliced salami or pepperoni

Grated mozzarella cheese or cheddar

- Split muffin in half. Spread muffin with canned pizza sauce.
- Add salami or pepperoni.
- Top with grated cheese and place under grill until cheese melts and begins to bubble.

If you want to go all out, you can add any combination of the following ingredients: cooked chopped onion, cooked chopped green pepper, sliced jalapeno peppers, and chopped green or black olives.

Jack Quesadillas

$^1/_2$ cup ricotta cheese

6 (15 cm) corn tortillas

$^2/_3$ cup shredded mild cheddar cheese

120 g marinated green capsicum chopped and mixed with $^1/_2$ teaspoon chilli powder

- Spread about 1 tablespoon ricotta over tortilla. Sprinkle with 1 heaped tablespoon of cheese and 1 tablespoon of green capsicum. Place a second tortilla on top.
- Repeat to make 2 more quesadillas.
- In a heated skillet add 1 quesadilla and cook 3 minutes on each side. Remove from heat and cut into 4 wedges. Repeat with remaining quesadillas.

Serve warm with salsa.

Toasted Pepperoni

1 box melba toasts

$^3/_4$ cup chilli sauce

150 g pepperoni, thinly sliced

1 cup shredded mozzarella cheese

- Spread toast with chilli sauce and top with pepperoni slices.
- Sprinkle with cheese and bake on cookie sheet at 190°C for 3 to 5 minutes.

Cocktail Sausages

$^2/_3$ cup prepared mustard

1 cup plum jam

$^1/_2$ teaspoon garlic powder

450 g cocktail frankfurts

- Mix mustard, jam and garlic powder. Heat.
- Add frankfurts; heat thoroughly and serve hot.

Green Eyes

4 dill pickles or pickled cucumbers

4 slices sandwich ham

Light cream cheese, softened

Black pepper

- Dry off pickles.
- Lightly coat one side of the ham slices with cream cheese and sprinkle on a little pepper.
- Roll the pickle up in the ham slice coated with cream cheese.
- Chill. Slice into circles to serve.

Cheddar Cheese Ring

2 (500 g) packets shredded cheddar cheese

1 small onion, finely chopped

1 cup mayonnaise

1½ cups finely chopped pecans plus 2 tablespoons for garnish

- Combine cheese, onion, mayonnaise and pecans. Press into a 20-cm ring mould.
- Cover with plastic wrap and refrigerate until set. Unmould when firm.
- Sprinkle top of cheese ring with additional chopped pecans.
- Slice to serve on wheat crackers.

Bacon-Oyster Bites

1 (140 g) can smoked oysters, drained, chopped

⅔ cup herb-seasoned stuffing mix

¼ cup water

8 slices bacon, halved and partially cooked

- Combine oysters, stuffing mix and water. Add another teaspoon water if mixture seems too dry.
- Form into balls, using about 1 tablespoon mixture for each. Wrap a half slice of bacon around each and secure with a toothpick.
- Place on a rack in a shallow baking pan. Cook at 180°C for 25 to 30 minutes.

Cheese in the Round

1 cup grated cheddar cheese

120 g margarine, softened

$1^{1}/_{4}$ cups flour

$^{1}/_{2}$ teaspoon cayenne pepper

- Combine all ingredients and form rolls $2^{1}/_{2}$ cm in diameter. Wrap in plastic wrap and chill.
- When ready to bake, slice into 7 mm thick rounds and bake at 190°C for 5 to 8 minutes.

Garlic Prawns

1 clove garlic, crushed

$^{2}/_{3}$ cup chilli sauce

250 g thin bacon strips

500 g medium prawns, cooked

- Add garlic to chilli sauce and set aside for several hours.
- Grill the bacon on one side only. Cut in half.
- Dip prawns in the chilli sauce and then wrap with half a bacon strip on the uncooked side out; fasten with toothpicks. Refrigerate.
- Just before serving, grill prawns until bacon is crisp.

Special Pimento Cheese

5 cups shredded sharp cheddar cheese

2 (120 g) jars diced pimentos, drained

1 cup salsa

3 tablespoons mayonnaise

- Combine grated cheese, pimentos and salsa in large bowl.
- Stir in mayonnaise, blending well. Store in refrigerator.

Homemade Pimento Cheese

2 cups grated cheddar cheese

1/2 cup salad dressing (not mayonnaise)

2 tablespoons pimento, chopped

1/4 teaspoon white vinegar

- Combine and mix together all the ingredients. Chill several hours, if possible, before serving. Serve on crackers.

Bacon Nibblers

1 (500 g) packet sliced bacon, at room temperature

1 1/2 cups brown sugar

1 1/2 teaspoons dry mustard

1/4 teaspoon black pepper

- Cut each slice of bacon in half. Combine the brown sugar, dry mustard and black pepper in a shallow bowl.
- Dip each half slice of bacon in brown sugar mixture, pressing down so the bacon is well coated. Place each slice on a baking sheet with sides.
- Bake at 150°C for 25 minutes, turning once, until bacon is browned. Immediately remove with tongs to several layers of paper towels. Bacon will harden and can be broken in pieces.

Holy Guacamole

4 avocados, peeled

1/2 cup salsa

1/4 cup sour cream

1 teaspoon salt

- Split avocados and remove seeds. Mash avocados with a fork.
- Add salsa, sour cream and salt.

Serve with tortilla chips.

Great Balls of Fire

1 (450 g) pepperoni, sliced

3 green onions, chopped

1 (415 g) can diced tomatoes with onion, garlic and basil

1 (1 kg) box processed cheddar cheese, cubed

- Saute pepperoni in a large skillet. Drain off fat. Add diced tomatoes.
- Add cheese to pepperoni mixture; cook on low heat until cheese melts. Serve hot in chafing dish (candleburner) with large potato crisps.

Prawn Squares Deluxe

1 (200 g) can prawns, drained, chopped

1 cup mayonnaise

1 cup shredded cheddar cheese

10–12 slices white bread, trimmed and cut in squares

- Combine the prawns, mayonnaise and cheese.
- Spread prawn mixture on the bread squares and grill until bubbly.

Prawn-Stuffed Eggs

8 hardboiled eggs

¼ cup mayonnaise

1 (200 g) can tiny prawns, drained

2 tablespoons sweet pickle relish, drained

- Cut eggs in half lengthwise; remove yolks, set aside the egg whites. In small bowl, mash egg yolks with mayonnaise.
- Add prawns and pickle relish and mix well. Refill egg whites. Refrigerate.

Chilli-Cheese Bites

6 slices white sandwich bread

1 cup shredded cheddar cheese

120 g butter, softened

3/4 teaspoon chilli powder

- Trim crusts from bread and cut each slice into 4 squares.
- Combine cheese, margarine and chilli powder and mix well.
- Place heaped teaspoonful of mixture on each bread square; place on baking sheet. Bake at 190°C for 10 minutes or until puffy and lightly browned.

Whiz Biz

1 (250 g) jar processed cheese spread

2 tablespoons dry white wine (or cooking wine)

1 teaspoon prepared mustard

1 teaspoon worcestershire sauce

- Mix all ingredients together. Chill. Serve with crackers.

Water Chestnut Dip

1 (250 g) can sliced water chestnuts, chopped

1 cup chopped pecans

1 (600 mL) carton sour cream

1 (35 g) envelope leek or onion soup mix

- In a large bowl combine water chestnuts, pecans and the sour cream and mix well.
- Fold in the leek soup mix and mix well. Refrigerate.

Serve with wheat crackers.

Cucumber Squares

1 (250 g) packet cream cheese, softened

1 teaspoon chopped fresh dill

3 medium cucumbers, peeled, grated

1 envelope dry ranch salad dressing mix

- In mixing bowl, combine cream cheese and dill weed and beat until creamy.
- Fold in grated cucumbers and ranch dressing.
- Spread on pumpernickel or rye bread slices.

Artichoke Bites

$1^1/_2$ cups mayonnaise

$^3/_4$ cup freshly grated parmesan cheese

1 tablespoon chopped green chilli

1 (400 g) can artichoke hearts, chopped

- Mix mayonnaise, parmesan cheese, green chillies and artichoke hearts. (Remove any spikes or tough leaves from artichokes.)
- Put 1 teaspoon of the mixture on bite-size toast rounds. Grill until lightly brown.

Bacon-Wrapped Water Chestnuts

1 (250 g) can whole water chestnuts, drained

$^1/_4$ cup soy sauce

$^1/_4$ teaspoon cayenne pepper

About 250 g bacon, cut in thirds

- Marinate water chestnuts for 1 hour in soy sauce.
- Wrap $^1/_3$-slice bacon around the water chestnuts and fasten with a toothpick.
- Bake at 190°C for 20 minutes or until bacon is done. Drain and serve hot.

No-See-Um Chicken Livers

2 white onions, sliced

10–12 chicken livers

4 strips bacon

$^1/_3$ cup sherry

- Place onion slices in shallow pan. Top each onion slice with a chicken liver and $^1/_3$-strip bacon. Pour sherry over all.
- Bake uncovered at 180°C for about 45 minutes or until bacon is crisp. Baste occasionally with pan drippings.

Border Queso

2 canned jalapeno peppers, reserve 1 tablespoon liquid

1 (500 g) box processed cheddar cheese

1 (120 g) jar pimentos, drained and chopped

3 fresh green onions (shallots), chopped

- Seed jalapeno peppers and chop.
- Combine peppers, cheese, pimentos and onion in saucepan.
- Heat on stove, stirring constantly, until cheese melts. Stir in reserved liquid. Serve with tortilla chips.

Toasted Crab

$^3/_4$ cup shredded cheddar cheese

120 g margarine, softened

1 (170 g) can crabmeat, drained and flaked

6 English muffins, halved

- In a bowl, combine cheese, softened margarine and crabmeat and mix well.
- Spread mixture on each muffin half. Cut each muffin into quarters and place on baking sheet.
- Grill for 5 minutes. Serve hot.

Bubbly Franks

1 (250 g) packet frankfurts

$^{1}/_{2}$ cup chilli sauce

$^{1}/_{2}$ cup packed brown sugar

$^{1}/_{2}$ cup whisky

- Cut frankfurts into bite-size pieces.
- Combine chilli sauce, sugar and whisky in a saucepan.
- Add frankfurts to sauce and simmer 30 minutes. Serve in chafing dish (candleburner).

Cheese Straws

$^{1}/_{2}$ (375 g) packet pastry crust mix

$^{3}/_{4}$ cup shredded cheddar cheese

Cayenne pepper

$^{1}/_{4}$ teaspoon garlic powder

- Prepare pastry crust mix according to packet directions. Roll out into a rectangular shape.
- Sprinkle cheese over dough and press the cheese into the dough.
- Sprinkle cayenne pepper over the cheese.
- Fold dough over once to cover cheese. Roll out with rolling pin to make a $^{1}/_{2}$-cm thickness.
- Cut dough into 1 cm by 7.5 cm strips and place on a lightly greased baking sheet.
- Bake at 180°C for 12 to 15 minutes.

Cheddar Toppers

1 cup chopped black olives

1 cup shredded cheddar cheese

$^1/_2$ cup mayonnaise

$^1/_2$ cup finely chopped green olives

- Combine all ingredients and mix well.
- To serve, spread mixture on English muffins. Bake at 180°C for 30 minutes. After baking, quarter the muffins and serve as hors d'oeuvres.

Tortilla Rollers

1 (250 g) packet cream cheese, softened

1 (200 g) jar chopped black olives, drained

$^1/_2$ (250 g) jar jalopino chilli, drained and chopped

1 (375 g) jar salsa

- With a mixer, beat cream cheese until smooth. Add black olives, green chillies and $^1/_4$ cup salsa, mixing well.

To serve, spread on flour tortillas and roll up. Refrigerate several hours. Slice in half-inch slices. Insert toothpick in each slice and dip in salsa.

Cheese It

1 (125 g) jar processed cheese spread, softened

60 g butter, softened

$^1/_2$ cup flour

$^1/_4$ teaspoon salt

- In mixer whip the cheese and butter, mixing flour and salt. Make a roll $3^1/_2$ cm in diameter; place in freezer for 15 to 20 minutes.
- When chilled slice 1 cm thick to make small circles.
- Place on ungreased baking sheet and bake at 220°C for 12 to 15 minutes.

Onion Crisps

240 g butter, softened

2 cups shredded cheddar cheese

1 (30 g) packet dry onion soup mix

2 cups flour

- Combine all ingredients. Dough will be very thick.
- Divide into two batches and form into two rolls. Refrigerate for about 3 hours.
- Slice in $^1/_2$-cm thick slices.
- Bake at 180°C for 12 to 15 minutes.

Pepperoni Pinwheels

$2^1/_2$ cups scone mix

$^2/_3$ cup milk

450 g pepperoni, chopped

1 green or red capsicum, seeded and cut

- In medium bowl. Combine scone mix and milk and mix well.
- Divide dough into 3 parts. Roll each piece of dough into a thin rectangle.
- Place chopped pepperoni and capsicum pieces in a food processor and process until minced. Spread on each dough rectangle and pat down.
- Roll up like a Swiss roll. Cover with foil and chill overnight. Slice into thin slices and bake at 190°C for 15–20 minutes.

Sausage Bites

500 g pepperoni

450 g colby or cheddar cheese, grated

$3^3/_4$ cups scone mix

$^1/_2$ teaspoon garlic powder

- Combine pepperoni, cheese, garlic powder and scone mix. Kneed thoroughly.
- Roll into $2^1/_2$-cm balls.
- Bake on a cookie sheet at 180°C for 15 to 18 minutes until lightly browned.

Hot Cocktail Squares

2 small green chillies, seeded and chopped

100 g diced bacon bits

1 (500 g) packet shredded cheddar cheese

7 eggs

- In a greased 18 × 28 cm baking dish, layer green chillies, bacon bits and cheese.
- Beat eggs with a fork until well beaten. Season with a little salt and several drops Tabasco. Pour over cheese.
- Bake covered at 180°C for 25 minutes. Uncover and bake another 10 minutes. Cut into squares. Serve warm.

Mexican Fudge

1 (500 g) packet shredded mild cheddar cheese

4 eggs, beaten

2/3 cup jalapeno green sauce

1 teaspoon worcestershire sauce

- In an oil sprayed 18 × 28 cm baking dish, spread half of the cheese in the dish.
- Combine eggs with green sauce and worcestershire sauce and pour over cheese in the dish. Add the remaining cheese.
- Bake at 180°C for 30 minutes.
- Cut into squares to serve. May be served hot or room temperature.

Devil's Spread

1 (125 g) can devilled ham spread

3/4 cup mayonnaise

1 tablespoon grated onion

1/2 (250 g) jar pickled jalapeno slices, drained and chopped

- Mix all ingredients. Spread on wheat crackers.

Crispy Chestnuts

1 (250 g) can whole water chestnuts

5–6 slices bacon, quartered

Honey mustard

- Wrap each water chestnut with quartered strip of bacon. Secure with toothpick.
- Grill until bacon is cooked and remove.
- Dip in honey mustard.

Peanut Butter Sticks

1 loaf thin sliced sandwich bread

1 cup smooth peanut butter

$^1/_2$ cup peanut oil

1 teaspoon sugar, optional

- Trim crust from the bread. Cut each slice into four fingers. Place bread and the bread crust in separate pans.
- Bake at 100°C for 1 hour or until crisp, turning often.
- In your food processor make crumbs from the dry bread crust.
- Mix peanut butter and oil. Dip bread fingers into peanut mixture, then roll in breadcrumbs.
- Arrange in layers in an airtight container; let stand overnight. These must be stored in a tightly covered container.

Hot Artichoke Spread

1 (420 g) can artichoke hearts, drained, finely chopped

1 cup mayonnaise

1 cup grated parmesan cheese

1 teaspoon each crushed garlic and dried oregano

- Remove the tough outer leaves, and chop artichoke hearts. Combine all ingredients, mixing thoroughly.
- Pour into a 23-cm square baking pan.
- Bake at 180°C for 20 minutes.

Serve hot with assorted crackers.

Artichoke Spread

1 (400 g) jar marinated artichoke hearts

1 cup grated parmesan cheese

1 cup mayonnaise

1 teaspoon dried parsley

- Drain artichoke hearts and chop. Combine artichokes, cheese, mayonnaise and parsley, blending well.
- Spoon into a non-stick sprayed 23-cm baking dish. Bake at 180°C for 20 minutes.

Serve with melba toast rounds.

Smoky Gouda Spread

3/4 cup chopped walnuts

1 (250 g) smoked gouda cheese

1 (250 g) packet cream cheese, softened

1/4 cup sliced green onions (shallots)

- Spread walnuts in a shallow baking pan. Bake at 160°C for 10 minutes or until lightly toasted. Cool and set aside.
- Trim and discard outer red edge of gouda cheese. Grate cheese. With mixer combine the cream cheese and gouda cheese. Mixing well, stir in walnuts and onions.

Serve with apple wedges or crackers.

Jiffy Tuna Spread

1 (200 g) can white tuna, drained

$^1/_2$ cup chopped ripe olives

1 teaspoon each crushed garlic and dried oregano

1 (300 mL) carton sour cream

- Combine all ingredients, mixing well. Sprinkle with a little paprika for colour and serve with crackers.

Creamy Cucumber Spread

1 cup seeded, chopped cucumber

1 (250 g) packet cream cheese, softened

$^1/_2$ cup mayonnaise

1 teaspoon seasoned salt

- Before chopping cucumber, make sure seeds have all been removed.
- With mixer, beat cream cheese until creamy; mix in mayonnaise, seasoned salt and cucumber.

Spread on crackers.

Cucumber-Garlic Dip

2 unpeeled cucumbers

1 (500 g) packet cream cheese, softened

2 tablespoons lemon juice

2 cloves garlic, crushed

- With a grater, coarsely grate both cucumbers, reserving juice.
- In mixer bowl, combine cream cheese, lemon juice and garlic. Beat until cream cheese is fairly smooth.
- Thin mixture with reserved cucumber juice as needed. Add salt to taste. Cover and refrigerate.

Serve with vegetable sticks.

Olive-Cheese Appetisers

1 cup pimento-stuffed olives, chopped

2 fresh green onions, finely chopped

$1\frac{1}{2}$ cups shredded mild cheddar cheese

$\frac{1}{2}$ cup mayonnaise

- In large bowl, combine all ingredients and mix well.
- Spread on English muffins and bake at 190°C until bubbly.
- Cut muffins into quarters and serve hot.

Black Olive Spread

1 (250 g) packet cream cheese, softened

$\frac{1}{2}$ cup mayonnaise

4 tablespoons finely chopped black olives

3 green onions (shallots), chopped very fine

- Cream together the cream cheese and mayonnaise until smooth.
- Add olives and onions. Chill.

Spread on slices of party rye.

Pineapple-Island Spread

2 (250 g) packets cream cheese, softened

1 (300 mL) carton sour cream

1 (250 g) can crushed pineapple, drained

$\frac{1}{2}$ cup finely chopped pecans

- In mixer bowl, combine cream cheese and sour cream and beat until creamy.
- Fold in pineapple, juice and pecans and mix well. Refrigerate.

Spread on banana nut bread, zucchini bread or use as a fruit dip.

Caramel Apple Dip

1 (250 g) packet cream cheese, softened

1 cup packed brown sugar

1 teaspoon vanilla

½ cup chopped dry roasted peanuts

- Combine cream cheese, brown sugar and vanilla with mixer. Beat until creamy. Stir in peanuts. Refrigerate.

Serve with crisp apple slices.

Nutty Apple Dip

1 (250 g) packet cream cheese, softened

1 cup packed brown sugar

1 teaspoon vanilla

1 cup finely chopped pecans

- In a small mixing bowl combine cream cheese, sugar and vanilla. Beat until smooth.
- Stir in pecans.

Serve with sliced apples for dipping.

Orange Dip for Apples

1 (250 g) packet cream cheese, softened

1 (200 g) carton orange yoghurt

½ cup orange marmalade

¼ cup finely chopped pecans

- In mixing bowl beat cream cheese until smooth.
- Fold in remaining ingredients. Refrigerate.

Serve with apple slices.

Orange-Sour Cream Dip

200 ml orange concentrate

1 (100 g) packet vanilla instant pudding mix

1 cup milk

$^1/_4$ cup sour cream

- Combine the orange juice concentrate, vanilla pudding mix and milk. Stir with a wire whisk until mixture is blended and smooth. Stir in sour cream.
- Cover and chill at least 2 hours.

Serve with fresh fruit.

Chocolate Fruit Dip

1 (250 g) packet cream cheese, softened

$^1/_4$ cup chocolate syrup

1 (213 g) jar marshmallow spread

Fruit

- In a mixing bowl beat cream cheese and chocolate syrup until smooth.
- Fold in marshmallow spread.
- Cover and refrigerate until serving.

Serve with apple wedges, banana chunks or strawberries.

Juicy Fruit Dip

1 (250 g) packet cream cheese, softened

1 (213 g) jar marshmallow spread

$^1/_4$ teaspoon ground ginger

- Cream together with the mixer, the cream cheese and marshmallow spread; fold in ginger.
- Chill.

Serve with apple slices, pineapple sticks, honeydew slices, etc.

Peanut Butter Spread

1 (250 g) packet cream cheese, softened

1²/₃ cups creamy peanut butter

¹/₂ cup powdered sugar

1 tablespoon milk

- In mixer, cream together all ingredients.

Serve spread with apple wedges or crackers.

Fruit Dip for Nectarines

1 (250 g) packet cream cheese, softened

2 (213 g) jars marshmallow spread

¹/₄ teaspoon cinnamon

¹/₈ teaspoon ground ginger

- With mixer, combine and beat together all ingredients. Mix well. Refrigerate.

Serve with unpeeled slices of nectarines or any other fruit.

Sweet and Creamy Fruit Dip

1 (300 mL) carton sour cream

3 heaped tablespoons brown sugar

¹/₂ teaspoon ground cinnamon

Dash ground ginger

- Mix sour cream, brown sugar and cinnamon.
- Serve with fresh fruit.

Amaretto Dip Spread

1 (250 g) packet cream cheese, softened

$^1/_4$ cup amaretto liqueur

$^1/_4$ cup chopped slivered almonds, toasted

Banana bread

- With mixer, blend cream cheese and amaretto. Stir in the toasted almonds. Serve with crackers or sliced apples.

This is also a good spread on banana bread, zucchini bread, etc.

Devilled Pecans

60 g butter, melted

1 tablespoon worcestershire sauce

2 cups pecan halves

$^1/_4$ teaspoon cayenne pepper

- In a mixing bowl combine the butter and the worcestershire sauce and mix well.
- Add pecans, pepper and $^1/_4$ teaspoon salt. Stir and toss pecans until well coated.
- Roast on baking tray at 180°C for 15 minutes, stirring or shaking the pan occasionally.

Classy Red Pecans

60 g butter

$1^1/_2$ teaspoons chilli powder

$^3/_4$ teaspoon garlic salt

3 cups pecan halves

- In large skillet, melt butter. Stir in chilli powder, garlic salt and pecans.
- Cook on medium heat, stirring pecans constantly for 4 or 5 minutes until browned and well coated with chilli powder.

Cinnamon Pecans

500 g shelled pecan halves

1 egg white, slightly beaten with fork

2 tablespoons cinnamon

$^3/_4$ cup sugar

- Combine the pecan halves with the egg white and mix well.
- Sprinkle with mixture of the cinnamon and sugar. Stir until all pecans are coated.
- Spread on a baking tray and bake at 160°C for about 20 minutes. Cool. Store in a covered container.

Toasted Pecans

12 cups pecan halves

120 g margarine

Salt

$^1/_2$ teaspoon garlic powder

- Place pecans in a large baking pan. In 120°C oven, toast pecans for 30 minutes to dry.
- Add margarine and melt in baking pan. Let pecans get completely greasy, stirring twice.
- After pecans and margarine have mixed well, sprinkle with salt and garlic powder and stir often.
- Toast pecans one hour more until margarine has been absorbed. Pecans will crisp on cooling.

Sugar-Coated Peanuts

$1^1/_2$ cups sugar

1 tablespoon maple flavouring

$4^1/_2$ cups raw shelled peanuts

$1^1/_2$ teaspoons salt

- In a large saucepan combine the sugar, $^3/_4$ cup water, maple flavouring and peanuts. Stir over medium heat for 20 minutes or until almost all of the liquid is absorbed.
- Spread on a greased 25 × 38 cm baking tray and sprinkle with salt. Bake at 180°C for about 25 minutes or until peanuts are well coated, stirring 2 to 3 times.
- Remove to a wax paper-lined baking sheet to cool. Store in airtight container.

Best Tropical Punch

1 (850 mL) can pineapple juice

1 (850 mL) can apricot nectar

300 mL limeade concentrate

2 (1.25 litre) bottles ginger ale, chilled

- Combine the first three juices and refrigerate. When ready to serve, add ginger ale. Makes $4^1/_2$ litres.

Easiest Grape Punch

1 (1.25 litre) bottle ginger ale

300 g red seedless grapes

2 (750 mL) bottles sparkling white grape juice, chilled

- Freeze an ice ring of the ginger ale and seedless grapes.
- When ready to serve, pour sparkling white grape juice in punch bowl with ice ring. Makes $2^3/_4$ litres.

Sparkling white grape juice is great just by itself!

Great Fruit Punch

1 (each 850 mL and 425 mL) cans pineapple juice

1.3 litres apple juice

1.25 litres ginger ale

Fresh mint to garnish, optional

- Combine pineapple juice and apple juice and make an ice ring with part of the juice.
- Chill remaining juice and ginger ale.
- When ready to serve, combine juices and ginger ale and place ice ring in punch bowl. Makes 5 litres.

Perfect Party Punch

1 (375 mL) can coola lime concentrate

1 (1.5 litre) can pineapple juice, chilled

1 (1.5 litre) apricot nectar, chilled

1 (1.2 litre) ginger ale, chilled

- Dilute the lime concentrate as directed on the can.
- Add the pineapple juice and apricot nectar, stirring well.
- When ready to serve, add the ginger ale. Makes $4^{1}/_{2}$ litres.

Ruby Red Punch

1 (each 850 g and 425 g) cans pineapple and grapefruit juice

$^{1}/_{2}$ cup sugar

$^{1}/_{4}$ cup cinnamon candies

1.2 litre ginger ale, chilled

- In a large saucepan, combine pineapple and grapefruit juice, sugar and candies. Bring to the boil, stirring until candies are dissolved.
- Cool until time to serve, stirring occasionally, to completely dissolve candies.
- Add ginger ale just before serving. Makes 3 litres.

Cranberry Punch

1 (1.2 litre) bottle ginger ale, chilled

1 (1.5 litre) can pineapple juice, chilled

1 litre cranberry juice, chilled

1 litre pineapple sorbet, broken up

- Pour all ingredients in punch bowl. Serve. Makes 4.7 litres.

Creamy Strawberry Punch

1 (300 g) packet frozen strawberries, thawed

2 litres strawberry ice cream, softened

2 (2 litre) bottles ginger ale, chilled

Fresh strawberries to garnish, optional

- Process strawberries through blender.
- Combine strawberries, chunks of ice cream and the ginger ale in punch bowl.
- Stir and serve immediately. Makes approx. 6 litres.

Mocha Punch

4 cups brewed coffee

$^1/_4$ cup sugar

4 cups milk

4 cups chocolate ice cream, softened

- In a container, combine coffee and sugar; stir until sugar is dissolved. Refrigerate for 2 hours.
- Just before serving, pour into a small punch bowl.
- Add milk; mix well. Top with scoops of ice cream and stir well. Makes $1^1/_2$ litres.

Party-Hardy Punch

1 (each 850 g and 425 g) cans pineapple juice

1.3 litres apple juice

2 (1.25 litre) bottles ginger ale, chilled

Pineapple chunks to garnish, optional

- Combine pineapple and apple juice in a very large plastic container or any container large enough to hold both juices. You can use two plastic pitchers. Freeze both juices.
- When ready to serve, place pineapple and apple juice in punch bowl and add the chilled ginger ale. Stir to mix. Makes 5 litres.

Cranberry-Lemon Punch

2 (1 litre) bottles cranberry juice

1 (200 mL) can lemonade concentrate

$^2/_3$ cup maraschino cherry juice

2 litres lemon lime soda, chilled

- Combine all ingredients.

It would be good to have ice ring made out of cranberry juice, lemon slices and maraschino cherries.

Makes 4.2 litres.

Pina Colada Punch

1 (each 850 mL and 425 mL) cans pineapple juice, chilled

1 (440 g) can crushed pineapple, undrained

1 (425 g) can thick coconut milk

1.2 litre bottle 7-Up, chilled

- Combine all ingredients.
- Serve over ice cubes.

Makes 3.3 litres.

Sparkling Wine Punch

6 oranges, unpeeled, thinly sliced

1 cup sugar

2 (750 mL) bottles dry white wine

3 (750 mL) bottles sparkling wine, chilled

- Place orange slices in a large plastic or glass container and sprinkle with sugar.
- Add white wine; cover and chill at least 8 hours.
- Stir in sparkling wine.

Champagne Punch

1 (750 mL) bottle champagne, chilled

1.2 litre bottle ginger ale, chilled

$^{2}/_{3}$ cup orange juice concentrate

Orange slices to garnish, optional

- Mix all ingredients in punch bowl. Serve chilled.

Makes 2 litres.

Apple Party Punch

1 (750 mL) bottle sparkling apple cider

2 cups apple juice

1 cup pineapple juice

$^{1}/_{2}$ cup brandy

- Combine all ingredients and freeze 8 hours.
- Remove punch from freezer 30 minutes before serving.
- Place in a small punch bowl and break into chunks. Stir until slushy.

Amaretto Cooler

$1^{1}/_{4}$ cups amaretto

1.8 litres cold orange juice

1 (450 mL) bottle club soda, chilled

Orange slices to garnish, optional

- Combine all ingredients, stirring well. Serve over ice.

Creamy Orange Drink

$1^3/_4$ cups milk

1 cup vanilla ice cream

$^1/_3$ cup orange juice concentrate

1 teaspoon non-dairy creamer (coffee mate)

- In blender, combine all ingredients.
- Blend until smooth.

Banana Split Float

2 ripe bananas, mashed

3 cups milk

1 (300 g) packet frozen sweetened strawberries, thawed

3 cups chocolate ice cream, divided

- Place bananas in blender and add milk, strawberries and 1 cup of the chocolate ice cream. Beat just until blended.
- Pour into tall, chilled glasses and top each with a scoop of chocolate ice cream.

Lemon-Banana Shake

200 mL lemonade concentrate

1 cup diced bananas

1 litre vanilla ice cream

3 cups milk

- In mixing bowl, combine lemonade concentrate and bananas. Beat until it is a heavy consistency.
- For each milk shake, add one scoop vanilla ice cream and $^1/_4$ cup of lemon-banana mixture in bottom of glass.
- Fill glass $^2/_3$ full of milk and stir until blended. Top it off with one or more scoops of ice cream.

Peanut Power Shake

2 bananas, cut up

1/2 cup orange juice concentrate

1/4 cup peanut butter

1/4 cup milk

- In blender container, combine all ingredients. Cover and blend until smooth.
- Add 1 cup of ice cubes, blending until smooth.

Purple Shakes

2 cups grape juice

1 cup milk

1/2 litre vanilla ice cream

2 tablespoons sugar, optional

- In blender combine all ingredients. Cover and blend at high speed for 30 seconds. Serve immediately.

Kahlua Frosty

1 cup kahlua

1/2 litre vanilla ice cream

1 cup cream

1/4 teaspoon almond extract

- In a blender, combine all ingredients and one heaped cup of ice cubes.
- Blend until smooth. Serve immediately.

Orange Lush

$^2/_3$ (500 mL) carton orange juice concentrate

$^1/_2$ litre cranberry juice

$^1/_2$ cup sugar

1 litre club soda

- Combine orange juice, cranberry juice and sugar, mixing thoroughly.
- Just before serving, pour into punch bowl and stir in the chilled club soda.

Fruit Smoothie

1 cup orange juice

1 ripe banana, peeled, thickly sliced

1 ripe peach, cut into chunks

1 cup strawberries

- Put the orange juice into a blender.
- Add the banana, peach, strawberries and 1 cup of ice cubes.
- Blend on high speed until liquefied.

Tropical Fruit Smoothie

2 (200 mL) cartons vanilla yoghurt

1 punnet fresh blueberries

1 cup fresh peach slices

$^1/_2$ (440 g) can pineapple chunks, drained

- Process all ingredients in a blender until smooth, stopping to scrape down sides.
- Serve immediately.

Pineapple-Strawberry Cooler

2 cups milk

1 (410 g) can crushed pineapple, chilled

1 cup vanilla ice cream

2 cups strawberry ice cream

- In a mixer bowl, combine milk, pineapple and vanilla ice cream.
- Mix just until blended. Pour into tall glasses and top with a scoop of strawberry ice cream.

Strawberry Smoothie

2 bananas, peeled, sliced

1 punnet fresh strawberries, quartered

1 (250 g) container strawberry yoghurt

$^1/_4$ cup orange juice

- Place all ingredients in blender. Process until smooth.

Orange Slush

2 cups orange juice

$^1/_2$ cup instant, non-fat dry milk

$^1/_4$ teaspoon almond extract

8 ice cubes

- Add all ingredients in blender and process on high until mixture is combined and thickened. Serve immediately.

Lemonade Tea

2 family-size tea bags

$^1/_2$ cup sugar

1 (250 g) bottle lemon squeeze

1 litre ginger ale, chilled

- Steep tea in 3 litres water; then mix with sugar and lemon squeeze.
- Add ginger ale just before serving.

Spiced Iced Tea

2 litres brewed tea

$^2/_3$ cup sugar

1 (375 g) can coola lime concentrate

1 litre ginger ale, chilled

- Combine tea, sugar and coola lime; chill.
- Just before serving, add the chilled ginger ale.

Frosted Chocolate Milk

$^1/_2$ litre coffee ice cream

$^1/_2$ cup chocolate syrup

$^1/_4$ cup instant coffee flakes

$1^1/_2$ litres milk, divided

- In a blender, beat ice cream, chocolate syrup, coffee and about half of the milk. Beat until well blended.
- Combine the remaining milk and chill before serving.
- Serve in frosted glasses.

Coffee Milk Shake

500 mL vanilla ice cream, divided

1/4 cup milk

1/2 cup chocolate coated toffee bits

- In blender combine half the ice cream and all the milk. Cover and blend until combined.
- Add remaining ice cream. Cover and blend until desired consistency.
- Add toffee bits and process briefly with on/off pulse to mix.

Chocolate-Yoghurt Malt

1 litre frozen vanilla yoghurt

1 cup chocolate milk

1/4 cup instant chocolate malted milk drink

Mini-chocolate chips, optional

- Process all ingredients in a blender until smooth, stopping to scrape sides.
- Serve immediately.
- Top with mini-chocolate chips.

Spanish Coffee

1 tablespoon sugar

4 cups hot, brewed coffee

3/4 cup kahlua

Sweetened whipped cream

- Stir sugar into hot coffee and add kahlua.
- Pour into 4 serving cups.
- Top with whipped cream.

Instant Cocoa Mix

1 (8 litre capacity) box dry milk powder

1 (450 g) jar non-dairy creamer (coffee mate)

1 (450 g) can instant chocolate flavoured drink mix

$1^1/_4$ cups icing sugar

- Combine all ingredients and store in an airtight container.
- To serve, use $^1/_4$ cup cocoa mix per cup of hot water.

Amaretto

3 cups sugar

450 mL vodka

3 tablespoons almond extract

1 tablespoon vanilla essence

- Combine sugar and $2^1/_4$ cups water in a large pan. Bring mixture to the boil.
- Reduce heat. Let simmer 5 minutes, stirring occasionally. Remove from stove.
- Add vodka, almond and vanilla extracts. Stir to mix.
- Store in airtight jar.

Hot Cranberry Cider

1 (1.5 litre) bottle cranberry juice

$^1/_2$ (500 mL) carton orange juice concentrate

2 cups water

$^1/_2$ teaspoon cinnamon

- Combine cranberry juice, orange juice and water in large saucepan. Bring to the boil to blend flavours.
- Add cinnamon, stirring well. Serve hot.

Peppermint Hot Chocolate

3 cups hot milk, divided
8 small chocolate peppermint patties
Pinch salt
1 cup cream

- Combine $^1/_2$ cup hot milk with chocolate peppermint patties, stirring well.
- Add pinch salt and remaining hot milk.
- Heat to simmering, but do not boil.
- Add the cream.

Spiced Coffee

1 cup instant coffee
4 teaspoons grated lemon peel
4 teaspoons ground cinnamon
1 teaspoon ground cloves

- In a small jar, combine all ingredients; cover tightly.
- For each serving, spoon 2 teaspoons of coffee mix into coffee cup and stir in $^3/_4$ cup boiling water. Sweeten to taste.

Mexican Coffee

1 ounce kahlua
1 cup hot black coffee
Ground cinnamon
Sweetened whipped cream

- Pour kahlua and coffee into a tall mug.
- Sprinkle with cinnamon and stir.
- Top with whipped cream. (You can substitute frozen whipped topping.)

Kid's Cherry Sparkler

2 (170 g) jars red maraschino cherries, drained

2 (170 g) jars green maraschino cherries, drained

$1\frac{1}{2}$ litres distilled water

1 (2 litre) bottle cherry 7-Up, chilled

- Place 1 red or green cherry in each compartment of 4 ice cube trays.
- Fill trays with distilled water; freeze for 8 hours. Serve soft drink over ice cubes.

Apricot Punch

1 (400 g) can apricot nectar

1 (170 mL) orange juice concentrate, undiluted

2 tablespoons lemon juice

1 (2 litre) bottle ginger ale, chilled

- Combine apricot nectar, orange juice concentrate, lemon juice and 1 cup water. Chill.
- When ready to serve, stir in ginger ale.

Chocolate Mint Fizz

$\frac{1}{4}$ cup white creme de menthe

$\frac{1}{4}$ cup creme de cocao

500 g vanilla ice cream

500 g chocolate ice cream

- Place liqueurs into blender container.
- Add ice cream gradually and blend until smooth after each addition.
- Pour into glasses and serve immediately.

BREADS, BREAKFAST and BRUNCH

Creamy Rich Scones

2 cups flour

3 teaspoons baking powder

$^1/_2$ teaspoon salt

1 (300 mL) carton whipping cream

- Combine flour, baking powder and salt.
- In mixer bowl, beat the whipping cream only until it holds a shape.
- Combine the flour mixture and cream; mix with a fork. Put dough on a lightly floured board and knead it for about 1 minute.
- Pat dough to a 2 cm thickness. Cut out scones with a small cutter.
- Place on baking sheet; bake at 190°C for about 12 minutes or until lightly brown.

Quick, Creamy Scones

$2^1/_2$ cups scone mix

$^1/_2$ pint whipping cream

- Mix scone mix and cream. Place on a floured board. Knead several times.
- Pat out to 1 cm thickness with a scone cutter.
- Bake at 190°C for 12 to 15 minutes or until lightly brown.

Drunk Scones

$3^1/_4$ cups scone mix

$^1/_4$ teaspoon salt

1 teaspoon sugar

$1^2/_3$ cups beer

- Combine all ingredients and spoon into 12 greased muffin cups.
- Bake at 220°C for 15 to 20 minutes until golden.

Sour Cream Scones

$^{1}/_{3}$ cup soda water

$^{1}/_{3}$ cup sour cream

$^{1}/_{2}$ tablespoon sugar

2 cups scone mix

- In a mixing bowl combine all ingredients stirring with a fork just until the dry ingredients are moistened.
- Turn bowl out onto lightly floured board and knead lightly several times.
- Roll dough into a $2^{1}/_{2}$-cm thickness and cut with a scone cutter.
- Place dough in a greased 23 × 33 cm baking pan. Bake at 220°C for 12 to 14 minutes or until golden brown.

Cream Cheese Scones

1 (250 g) packet cream cheese, softened

120 g margarine, softened

1 cup self-raising flour

- Beat cream cheese and margarine at medium speed with mixer for 2 minutes. Gradually add flour, beating at low speed, just until blended.
- Spoon dough into miniature muffin pans, filling $^{2}/_{3}$ full.
- Bake at 180°C for 15 minutes or until golden brown.

Garlic-Flavoured Scones

5 cups scone mix

1 cup shredded cheddar cheese

1 (410 g) can chicken broth

$1^1/_2$ teaspoons garlic powder

- Mix all ingredients to form a soft dough. Drop by heaping spoonfuls onto greased baking sheet.
- Bake at 220°C for 10 minutes or until slightly brown.

Maple Syrup Scones

$2^1/_4$ cups scone mix

$^2/_3$ cup milk

$1^1/_2$ cups maple syrup

- Combine scone mix and milk. Stir just until moistened. On a floured surface roll dough into 1-cm thickness. Cut with a 5-cm scone cutter.
- Pour syrup into a 18 × 28 cm baking dish. Place scones on top of syrup.
- Bake at 210°C for 13 to 15 minutes or until scones are golden brown.

Serve with breakfast.

Speedy Scones

6 tablespoons margarine

3 cups self-raising flour

1 cup milk

Butter

- Cut margarine into the flour with a pastry cutter or by hand. Add milk and mix until dough forms a ball. Knead until dough is smooth.
- Place on a sp. floured surface and flatten slightly. Cut with a floured scone cutter and place in a well greased pan, turning to grease both sides of the scones.
- Bake at 200°C for 10 to 12 minutes.

Hot Rich Scones

$1^1/_3$ cup self-raising flour

1 (300 mL) carton cream

2 tablespoons sugar

Butter for serving

- Combine flour, cream and sugar and stir until blended.
- Drop scones by teaspoon onto a greased baking sheet.
- Bake at 200°C for about 10 minutes or until lightly brown.
- Serve with plain or flavoured butters on pages 84 and 85.

Come and Get 'Em Drop Scones

2 cups self-raising flor

4 tablespoons mayonnaise

1 cup milk

Butter for serving

- Mix all ingredients and drop by spoonfuls on a baking sheet.
- Bake at 200°C until scones are golden brown.
- Serve with plain or flavoured butters on pages 84 and 85.

Date Scones

1 cup chopped dates

2 cups scone mix

$^1/_2$ cup grated cheddar cheese

$^3/_4$ cup milk

- Combine dates, scone mix and cheese.
- Add milk; stir well to a moderately soft dough. Drop by teaspoonful onto a greased baking sheet.
- Bake in a 200°C oven for 12 to 15 minutes. Serve hot.

Cream Cheese Biscuits

90 g cream cheese, softened

120 g butter, softened

1 cup self-raising flour

1/4 teaspoon salt, optional

- In mixer beat cream cheese and butter together. Add flour, mixing well.
- Roll out to 1-cm thickness and cut with a small biscuit cutter.
- Place on a greased baking sheet and bake at 180°C for 20 minutes or until lightly browned.

Hot Cheese Biscuits

1 small (50 g) jar cheese spread

60 g margarine, softened

1/2 cup flour

1/8 teaspoon salt

- Mash cheese spread and the margarine, mixing well. Add flour and salt.
- Mix well. Roll into small balls. Chill 1 hour.
- Place on ungreased baking sheet.
- Bake at 200°C for 10 minutes. Balls will flatten as they cook. Serve hot.

Sausage-Cheese Scones

1 (250 g) packet grated cheddar cheese

500 g pork sausage mince

2 cups scone mix

3/4 cup milk

- Combine cheese, sausage mince and scone mix and milk.
- Drop on ungreased baking sheet.
- Bake at 200°C until lightly brown. Serve hot.

Strawberry Topping for Scones

$3^1/_2$ cups sugar

1 (300 g) carton frozen strawberries, thawed

$^2/_3$ cup orange juice concentrate

2 tablespoons lemon juice

- Combine sugar and strawberries in a large saucepan, mixing well. Over high heat bring to a full rolling boil. Boil one minute, stirring constantly.
- Remove from heat and stir in orange juice concentrate and lemon juice. Return to heat and bring to the boil for one minute, stirring constantly.
- Skim off foam off top. You could add red food colouring if you like.
- Pour into jelly glasses and seal with hot paraffin.

This is delicious over hot scones.

French Onion Scones

2 cups scone mix

$^1/_4$ cup milk

1 (250 g) container French onion dip

2 tablespoons finely chopped green onion

- Mix all ingredients together until soft dough forms. Drop dough onto a greased baking sheet.
- Bake at 200°C for about 10 minutes or until light golden brown.

Toasted French Bread

1 unsliced loaf French bread

125 g butter, softened

$^3/_4$ cup parmesan cheese

$1^1/_2$ teaspoons Tabasco

- Slice bread in half lengthwise, then quarter.
- Combine butter, parmesan cheese and Tabasco. Spread on top of slices using all the mixture. Place on baking sheet.
- Cook at 150°C for about 25 minutes or until heated thoroughly and browned on top.

Parmesan Bread Deluxe

1 loaf unsliced Italian bread

$^1/_2$ cup creamy Caesar salad dressing

$^1/_3$ cup grated parmesan cheese

3 tablespoons finely chopped green onions

- Cut 24 (1-cm thick) slices from bread. Reserve remaining bread for other use.
- In small bowl, combine dressing, cheese and onion. Spread a teaspoon of dressing mixture onto each bread slice.
- Place bread on baking sheet. Grill 10 cm from heat until golden brown. Serve warm.

Bacon-Cheese French Bread

1 (400 g) loaf unsliced French Bread

5 slices bacon, cooked, crumbled

250 g mozzarella cheese, shredded

125 g margarine, melted

- Slice loaf of bread into $2^1/_2$-cm slices. Place sliced loaf on a large piece of aluminium foil.
- Combine bacon and cheese. Sprinkle bacon and cheese in between slices of bread.
- Drizzle margarine over loaf, letting some drip down in between slices. Wrap loaf tightly in foil. Bake at 180°C for 20 minutes or until thoroughly heated. Serve hot.

Lemon Pepper French Bread

1 loaf unsliced French bread

120 g margarine, softened

$1^1/_2$ teaspoons lemon pepper

1 tablespoon mayonnaise

- Cut loaf in half horizontally. Blend margarine, lemon pepper and mayonnaise.
- Spread mixture on bread.
- Wrap bread in foil. Bake at 180°C for 15 minutes.

Cheese Bread

2 cups shredded sharp cheddar cheese

1 cup mayonnaise

1 packet salad dressing mix

10 (2.5 cm) slices French bread

- Combine cheese, mayonnaise and salad dressing mix.
- Spread on bread slices and heat in oven until brown.

Green Chilli and Cheese Bread

1 loaf Italian bread, unsliced

120 g margarine, melted

$^{1}/_{2}$ (250 g) jar jalapeno chilli slices, drained and chopped

$^{3}/_{4}$ cup grated cheddar cheese

- Slice bread almost all the way through.
- Combine melted margarine, chillies and cheese. Spread between bread slices.
- Cover loaf with foil. Bake at 180°C for 25 minutes.

Crunchy Bread Sticks

1 packet hot dog buns

250 g margarine, melted

1 teaspoon garlic powder

$^{1}/_{4}$ teaspoon paprika

- Take each half bun and slice in half lengthwise.
- Using a pastry brush, brush all bread sticks with melted margarine and sprinkle with garlic powder and paprika.
- Place on baking sheet and bake at 120°C for about 45 minutes.

Creamy Butter Bread

250 g salted butter, softened

2 cups self-raising flour

1 (300 mL) carton sour cream

- Combine all ingredients, mixing well.
- Drop by teaspoons into greased miniature muffin cups.
- Bake at 180°C for 20 minutes or until lightly browned.

Cheese Sticks

1 loaf thick sliced bread

125 g margarine, melted

1 cup grated cheddar cheese

1½ teaspoons paprika

- Remove crust from bread and slice into sticks.
- Brush or roll in melted margarine. Place on baking sheet.
- Sprinkle on parmesan and paprika.
- Bake at 150°C for 20 minutes.

Butter Rolls

2 cups scone mix

1 (300 mL) carton sour cream

125 g butter, melted

- Combine all ingredients and mix well. Spoon into greased muffin tins and fill only half full.
- Bake at 200°C for 12 to 14 minutes or lightly brown.

Tea Cakes

1 cup self-raising flour

1 cup cream

2 tablespoons sugar

⅛ teaspoon ground cinnamon

- Combine all ingredients and pour into greased mini-muffin cups.
- Bake at 190°C for 10 to 15 minutes.

Cheese Drop Scones

2 cups scone mix

$^2/_3$ cup milk

$^2/_3$ cup grated sharp cheddar cheese

60 g margarine, melted

- Spray baking sheet with non-stick spray.
- Mix together the scone mix, milk and cheese. Drop 1 heaped tablespoon of dough for each scone onto a greased baking sheet.
- Bake at 200°C for 10 minutes or until slightly browned.
- While warm, brush tops of scones with the melted margarine. Serve hot.

Corn Sticks

2 cups scone mix

1 (250 g) can creamed style sweet corn

2 tablespoons finely chopped green onion

Melted butter

- Mix scone mix, green onions and creamed corn together to form a dough.
- Place dough on a floured surface, roll out and cut into $7^1/_2 \times 2^1/_2$ cm strips. Brush with melted butter.
- Bake at 200°C for 15 to 16 minutes.

Mayo Muffins

$1^1/_4$ cups self-raising flour

3 tablespoons mayonnaise

1 cup whole milk

- Mix all ingredients together and spoon into greased muffin tins.
- Bake at 190°C for 20 minutes or until lightly browned.

Filled Muffins

1 box blueberry muffin mix with blueberries

1 egg

$^1/_3$ cup raspberry jam

$^1/_4$ cup almond flakes

- Rinse blueberries and drain.
- In bowl, combine the muffin mix, egg and $^1/_2$ cup water. Stir until moistened; break up any lumps in the mix.
- Place paper liners in 8 muffin cups. Fill cups half full of the batter.
- Combine the raspberry jam with the blueberries. Spoon mixture on top of batter. Cover with remaining batter. Sprinkle almond flakes over batter.
- Bake at 190°C for about 18 minutes or until lightly brown.

Ginger-Raisin Muffins

1 box gingerbread mix

$1^1/_4$ cups lukewarm water

1 egg

$^1/_2$ cup seedless raisins

- Combine gingerbread mix, water and egg, mixing well. Stir in raisins.
- Pour into greased muffin tins filled half full.
- Bake at 180°C for 20 minutes or when tested done with a toothpick.

Blueberry-Orange Muffins

1 packet blueberry muffin mix with blueberries

2 egg whites

1/2 cup orange juice

Orange marmalade

- Wash blueberries with cold water and drain.
- Mix together the muffin mix, egg whites and orange juice; break up any lumps. Fold blueberries gently into batter.
- Pour into muffin tins (with paper liners) about half full.
- Bake at 190°C for 18 to 20 minutes until toothpick inserted in centre comes out clean.
- Top with orange marmalade spooned over top of hot muffins.

Honey-Cinnamon Butter

250 g butter

1/2 cup honey

1 teaspoon ground cinnamon

Breakfast breads for serving

- Combine all ingredients in a small mixing bowl; beat until smooth.

Serve with muffins, toast, French toast or pancakes. Refrigerate any leftovers.

Orange Butter

$^{2}/_{3}$ cup butter, room temperature

$^{1}/_{4}$ cup orange juice concentrate

450 g icing sugar

1 teaspoon dried orange peel

- Blend all ingredients together in mixer. Store in refrigerator.

Great on biscuits and hot rolls.

Ambrosia Spread

1 (310 g) can mandarin orange sections, drained

1 (250 g) container soft cream cheese with pineapple, softened

$^{1}/_{4}$ cup flaked coconut, toasted

$^{1}/_{4}$ cup slivered almonds, chopped and toasted

- Chop orange sections; set aside.
- Combine cheese, coconut and almonds, blending well. Gently fold in orange sections. Refrigerate.
- Spread on date nut bread, banana bread, etc.

This can also be used as a dip for fruits.

Strawberry Butter

1 (300 g) packet frozen strawberries, undrained

1 cup unsalted butter, softened

1 cup icing sugar

Breakfast breads

- Place all ingredients in a food processor or mixer and process until well mixed.

Strawberry butter is delicious on scones, muffins or breads.

A Better Scramble

1 (35 g) packet cheese sauce mix

8 eggs, lightly beaten

2 tablespoons margarine

Snipped chives

- Put the eggs and a little bit of pepper into a bowl, mixing well.
- In a frying pan, melt the margarine. Pour in egg mixture and scramble over low heat until set.
- Sprinkle with chives.

Breakfast Wake-Up

12 eggs

1 (250 g) jar sliced jalapeno chillies

2 (500 g) packets shredded cheddar cheese

Salsa, optional

- Drain jalapeno chillies, saving juice.
- In a separate bowl, beat eggs with the chilli juice; add a little salt and pepper.
- Spray a 23 × 33 cm pan and spread half the cheese on bottom of pan and layer the chillies over this. Top with the remaining cheese.
- Pour eggs over the top and bake uncovered at 180°C for 45 minutes.

Cheesy Scrambled Eggs

2 tablespoons margarine

8 eggs

1 (250 g) jar sliced jalapeno chillies, drained

$^1/_2$ cup grated cheddar cheese

- Melt margarine in a frying pan.
- Beat remaining ingredients well, adding a little salt and black pepper; pour into pan.
- Cook and stir until set.

Creamy Eggs on Toast

50 g butter

4 level tablespoons flour

2 cups milk

6 hardboiled eggs, sliced

- Melt butter in a small saucepan; stir in flour. Gradually add milk, stirring.
- Cook over medium heat, stirring constantly until sauce is thickened.
- Gently fold in egg slices.

Serve over six slices toasted bread.

Baked Eggs

4 eggs

4 tablespoons cream

4 tablespoons cracker crumbs

4 tablespoons shredded cheddar cheese

- Grease 4 muffin cups and place 1 egg in each.
- Add 1 tablespoon each of cream, crumbs and cheese to each egg. Sprinkle with a little salt and pepper.
- Bake at 150°C for 12 to 20 minutes until eggs are set.

As many eggs as required may be prepared at the same time.

Mexican Eggs

4 corn tortillas

4 eggs

1 cup green chilli salsa

125 g grated sharp cheddar cheese

- Dip tortillas in heated oil in frying pan and remove quickly. Set tortillas on baking pan to keep warm.
- In skillet, fry eggs in a little butter until the whites are set. Place a fried egg on each tortilla.
- Heat salsa and spoon over each egg. Sprinkle grated cheese on top.
- Place baking pan under griller just until cheese melts. Serve hot.

Breakfast Tacos

4 eggs

4 flour tortillas

1 cup chopped, cooked ham

1 cup grated cheddar cheese

- Scramble eggs in frying pan.
- Lay tortillas flat and spoon eggs over the 4 tortillas.
- Sprinkle with ham and cheese. Roll up to enclose filling.
- Place tacos in a microwave-safe dish. Microwave for about 30 seconds or until cheese is melted. Serve immediately.

Glazed Bacon

500 g bacon

1/3 cup packed brown sugar

1 teaspoon flour

1/2 cup finely chopped pecans

- Arrange bacon slices close together, but not overlapping, on a wire rack over a drip pan.
- In a bowl, combine the brown sugar, flour and pecans; sprinkle evenly over the bacon.
- Bake at 180°C for about 30 minutes. Drain on paper towels.

Pecan Waffles

2 cups self-raising flour

1/2 cup oil

1/2 cup milk

2/3 cup finely chopped pecans

- Preheat waffle iron.
- In a bowl, combine flour, oil and milk. Beat until well mixed.
- Stir in chopped pecans.
- Pour approximately 3/4 cup batter into a hot waffle iron and bake until browned and crispy.

Waffle Flash

2 eggs

1 cup milk

$^1/_2$ teaspoon vanilla

8 slices stale bread

- Heat waffle iron according to directions.
- Beat eggs and slowly add milk and vanilla; beat well.
- Remove crust from bread and butter both sides of bread.
- When waffle iron is ready, dip bread in egg mixture and place in waffle iron. Close lid. Cook until lightly brown. Serve with syrup.

Light and Crispy Waffles

2 cups scone mix

1 egg

$^1/_2$ cup oil

$1^1/_3$ cups soda water

- Preheat waffle iron.
- Combine all ingredients in a mixing bowl and stir by hand.
- Pour just enough batter to cover waffle iron. Close lid and cook until light brown.

To freeze waffles. Freeze separately on baking sheet then place in a large plastic bag and seal. To heat, warm at 180°C for about 10 minutes.

Praline Toast

125 g butter, softened

1 cup packed brown sugar

$^1/_3$ cup finely chopped pecans

Bread slices

- Combine butter, sugar and pecans.
- Spread on bread slices.
- Toast in griller until brown and bubbly.

French Toast

4 eggs

1 cup cream

2 thick slices bread, cut into 3 strips each

Icing sugar

- Beat together eggs, cream and a pinch of salt.
- Dip bread into batter allowing batter to soak in.
- Fry bread in hot oil in a frying pan until brown; turn and fry on the other side.
- Transfer to baking sheet. Bake at 160°C for about 4 minutes or until puffed. Sprinkle with icing sugar.

Cinnamon Toast

$^2/_3$ cup sugar

1 heaped tablespoom cinnamon

Bread

Butter, softened

- Make cinnamon sugar by mixing sugar with cinnamon. Place in large salt or sugar shaker.
- Place bread on baking sheet and toast top by grilling under hot griller until light brown.
- Remove baking sheet and spread soft margarine on the toasted side. Sprinkle with cinnamon mixture.
- Return to griller and grill until tops are bubbly. Watch closely because sugar burns easily.

Sunrise Tacos

4 eggs, scrambled, divided

$^1/_2$ cup grated cheddar cheese, divided

$^1/_2$ cup salsa, divided

2 flour tortillas, divided

- For each taco, spread $^1/_2$ scrambled eggs, $^1/_4$ cup cheese and $^1/_4$ cup salsa on the tortilla and roll up.

Bacon and Egg Burrito

2 slices bacon, cooked, chopped

2 eggs, scrambled

$^{1}/_{4}$ cup shredded cheddar cheese

1 flour tortilla

- Sprinkle bacon, eggs and cheese in the middle of a tortilla. (Also add taco sauce or salsa, if you like.)
- Fold tortilla sides over and place seamside down on a dinner plate.
- Microwave for 30 seconds or just until heated thoroughly.

Hot Cheese Melt

1 (350 g) can whole jalapeno peppers, drained

1 (425 g) can diced tomatoes

1 (1 kg) box processed cheddar cheese

4 slices bacon, cooked crisp, crumbled

- Cut peppers in half and remove the seeds. Chop the peppers and place them in the bottom of a 23-cm pie plate.
- Spoon the diced tomatoes over the peppers. Cut the cheese into chunks and place them over the tomatoes.
- Bake at 150°C for about 15 minutes or until cheese melts. Let cheese set until room temperature. When ready to serve, sprinkle bacon over top.

Serve with tortilla chips.

Blueberry Coffee Cake

1 (455 g) packet blueberry muffin mix with blueberries

$^{1}/_{3}$ cup sour cream

1 egg

$^{2}/_{3}$ cup icing sugar

- Stir together the muffin mix, sour cream, egg and $^{1}/_{2}$ cup water.
- Rinse blueberries and gently fold into batter. Pour into a non-stick vegetable-sprayed 18 × 28 cm baking dish.
- Bake at 200°C for about 25 minutes.
- Mix powdered sugar and 1 tablespoon water and drizzle over coffee cake.

Sticky Pecan Rolls

2 (6 pack) packets round Cook at Home dinner rolls

4 tablespoons butter

2/3 cup packed brown sugar

24 pecan halves

- Place 1 roll in each of 12 well greased muffin cups.
- Cut an "x" in top of each roll.
- Combine the sugar and butter together and melt, mixing well. Spoon mixture over rolls.
- Tuck two pecan halves in the "x" on each roll. Bake at 180°C for 50 minutes or until slightly brown.

Corned Beef Hash Bake

2 (425 g) cans corned beef hash, slightly warmed

Margarine

6–8 eggs

1/3 cup cream

- Spread corned beef hash in a greased 23 × 33 cm pan. Pat down with the back of a spoon and make 6 to 8 deep hollows in the hash large enough to accommodate an egg.
- Fill hollows with tiny dab of margarine.
- Pour eggs into each hollow and cover the eggs with a tablespoon or so of the cream.
- Bake uncovered at 180°C for 15 to 20 minutes or until eggs are set as desired. Divide into squares to serve.

Dog Gones

10 day-old scones

2 cups canola oil

1 cup sugar

1 teaspoon cinnamon

- Cut each scone into 4 pieces.
- Heat shortening in frying pan and drop scone pieces in hot oil a few pieces at a time until golden brown. Remove and place on paper towels to drain.
- Dip in the mixture of sugar and cinnamon to coat well. Serve warm.

Cheese Enchiladas

1 dozen corn tortillas

1 (250 g) packet shredded cheddar cheese, divided

½ cup chopped onion, divided

2 (255 g) cans enchilada sauce

- Wrap tortillas in a slightly damp paper towel. Put between two salad plates and microwave on high for 45 seconds.
- Place ⅓ cup cheese and a sprinkle of onions on each tortilla; roll up. Place seam-side down in a 23 × 33 cm baking dish. Repeat with remaining tortillas.
- Pour enchilada sauce over enchiladas. Sprinkle with remaining cheese and onions.
- Cover and microwave on medium high for 5 to 6 minutes.

Pineapple-Brunch Slices

1 cup finely chopped ham

1 teaspoon mustard

2 tablespoons mayonnaise

5 slices pineapple, drained

- Combine ham, mustard and mayonnaise, mixing well.
- Spread on pineapple slices.
- Bake in an ungreased baking pan at 190°C for about 15 minutes or until heated thoroughly.

Chilli Rellenos

1 (250 g) jar jalapeno chilli slices, drained, chopped

1 (500 g) packet shredded mild cheddar cheese, divided

4 eggs, beaten

$^1/_2$ cup milk

- In a 18 × 28 cm baking dish, layer half the chillies, half the cheese, then the remaining chillies and cheese.
- Combine the eggs, milk and a little salt and pepper in a small bowl; mix well.
- Pour over the layers of cheese and chillies.
- Bake uncovered at 180°C for 30 minutes or until light brown and set. Cool for 5 minutes before cutting into squares.

Spiced Pears

1 (425 g) can pear halves

$^1/_3$ cup packed brown sugar

$^3/_4$ teaspoon ground nutmeg

$^3/_4$ teaspoon ground cinnamon

- Drain pears, reserving syrup. Set pears aside.
- Place syrup, brown sugar, nutmeg and cinnamon in a saucepan and bring to the boil. Reduce heat and simmer uncovered for 5 to 8 minutes stirring frequently.
- Add pears and simmer 5 minutes longer or until heated thoroughly.

Melon Boats

2 cantaloupes or rock melons, chilled

4 cups red and green seedless grapes, chilled

1 cup mayonnaise

$^1/_3$ cup concentrated orange juice, undiluted

- Prepare each melon in 6 lengthwise sections, removing seeds and peel. Place on separate salad plates on lettuce leaves.
- Heap grapes over and around the cantaloupe slices.
- Combine mayonnaise and juice concentrate; mixing well. Ladle over fruit.

Apricot Bake

4 (425 g) cans apricot halves, drained

1 (500 g) box light brown sugar, divided

2 cups Ritz cracker crumbs, divided

125 g butter, sliced

- Grease a 23 × 33 cm baking dish and line bottoms with 2 cans of drained apricots.
- Sprinkle half the brown sugar and half the cracker crumbs over apricots. Dot with half the butter.
- Repeat layers.
- Bake at 150°C for 1 hour.

Mini-Apricot Bake

2 (425 g) cans apricot halves, drained

$^3/_4$ cup packed brown sugar

1 cup Ritz cracker crumbs

125 g margarine, melted

- Butter a 2 litre casserole and layer apricots, sugar and cracker crumbs until all ingredients are used.
- Melt margarine and pour over casserole.
- Bake at 170°C for 35 minutes or until cracker crumbs are slightly brown. Serve hot or at room temperature.

Peachy Fruit Dip

1 (460 g) can sliced peaches, drained

1/2 cup marshmallow cream

1 (85 g) packet cream cheese, cubed

1/8 teaspoon ground nutmeg

- In a blender or food processor, combine all ingredients. Serve with assorted fresh fruit.

Gingered Cream Spread

1 (250 g) packet cream cheese, softened

120 g unsalted margarine, softened

2 tablespoons milk

3 tablespoons finely chopped crystallised ginger

- Combine all ingredients in mixer. Beat until creamy.
- Spread on your favourite fruit or nut breads.

Peach Bake

2 (460 g) cans peach halves, drained

1 cup packed brown sugar

1 cup Ritz cracker crumbs

120 g margarine, melted

- Butter a 2 litre casserole and layer peaches, sugar and cracker crumbs until all ingredients are used.
- Pour melted margarine over casserole. Bake at 150°C for 35 minutes or until cracker crumbs are slightly brown. Serve hot or at room temperature.

Bacon-Cheese Stromboli

1 large (130 cm) frozen pizza base, thawed

$^{3}/_{4}$ cup shredded cheddar cheese

$^{3}/_{4}$ cup shredded mozzarella cheese

6 bacon strips, cooked and crumbled

- Place pizza base on an ungreased baking sheet.
- On one half of the base, sprinkle cheeses and bacon to within $2^{1}/_{2}$ cm of edge. Brush dough edge with water.
- Fold base over filling; pinch edges to seal.
- Bake at 200°C for about 10 minutes or until golden. Serve with salsa.

Cut in pie slices.

Honey Butter

125 g butter, softened

$^{1}/_{4}$ cup honey

2 tablespoons lemon juice

1 tablespoon brown sugar

- With a hand mixer, cream the butter until fluffy and add honey in a fine stream.
- Add lemon juice and brown sugar, stirring until all ingredients are evenly blended.
- Chill until ready to serve.

Wonderful with hot scones!

Pineapple Coffee Cake

1 box butter cake mix

½ cup oil

4 eggs, slightly beaten

1 (410 g) can crushed pineapple

- In mixer, combine cake mix, oil and eggs. Beat until well mixed. Pour batter into a greased, floured 23 × 33 cm baking pan.
- Bake at 180°C for 45 to 50 minutes. Test with toothpick to make sure cake is done.
- With a knife, punch holes in cake about 5 cm apart. Spread crushed pineapple over cake while cake is still hot.

SOUPS, SALADS and SANDWICHES

Spicy Tomato Soup

2 (300 g) cans tomato soup

1 (415 g) can diced tomatoes with basil and garlic

Sour cream

250 g rashes bacon, fried until crisp, crumbled

- In a saucepan, combine soup and diced tomatoes and heat.
- To serve, place a dollop of sour cream on each bowl of soup and sprinkle crumbled bacon over sour cream.

Navy Bean Soup

3 cans navy beans, undrained

1 cup chopped ham

1 large onion, chopped

1/2 teaspoon garlic powder

- In large saucepan, combine beans, ham, onion and garlic powder.
- Add 1 cup water and bring to the boil. Simmer until onion is tender crisp.

Serve hot with cornbread.

Cream of Turkey Soup

1 (300 g) can cream of celery soup

1 (300 g) can cream of chicken soup

2 (300 g) cans milk or cream

1 cup finely diced chicken or turkey

- Combine all ingredients in a large saucepan.
- Serve hot.

Swiss Vegetable Soup

1 (50 g) packet dry vegetable soup mix

3 cups water

1 cup cream

$1^1/_2$ cups shredded Swiss cheese

- Combine soup mix and water in a saucepan and boil.
- Lower heat and simmer about 10 minutes.
- Add cream and cheese. Stir until cheese melts. Remove from heat; serve hot.

Bacon-Potato Soup

2 (410 g) cans chicken broth seasoned with garlic

2 potatoes, peeled, cubed

1 onion, finely chopped

6 strips bacon, cooked, crumbled

- In a large saucepan, combine broth, potatoes and onion. Bring to the boil; reduce heat to medium high and boil about 10 minutes or until potatoes are tender.
- Season with pepper.
- Ladle into bowls and sprinkle with crumbled bacon.

Tomato-French Onion Soup

1 (410 g) can tomato soup

2 (300 mL) cans French onion soup

Grated parmesan cheese

Croutons

- In saucepan combine soups and 2 soup cans of water. Heat thoroughly.
- Serve in bowls topped with croutons and a sprinkle of cheese.

Speedy Taco Soup

300 g chicken tenderloins, cut into chunks

1 (410 mL) can chicken consommé

1 (375 g) jar mild thick and chunky salsa

1 (400 g) can butter beans

- In large saucepan combine chicken, broth, salsa and beans. (A 400 g can of whole kernel corn could also be added.)
- Bring to the boil, reduce heat and simmer 15 minutes.

Spiked Crab Soup

1 packet dry onion soup mix

1 (170 g) can crabmeat, including liquid, flaked

1 (300 mL) carton cream

½ cup white wine

- Dissolve soup mix in 2 cups water.
- Add crabmeat, crab liquid and cream. Season with salt and pepper.
- Heat, but not to the boiling stage, and simmer for 20 minutes.
- Stir in wine; heat. Serve warm.

Crunchy Peanut Soup

2 (300 mL) cans cream of chicken soup

2 soup cans milk

1¼ cups crunchy peanut butter

½ teaspoon celery salt

- In a saucepan on medium heat, blend together the soup and milk.
- Stir in peanut butter and celery salt and heat until well blended.

New England Clam Chowder

1 (300 mL) can New England clam chowder
1 (300 mL) can cream of celery soup
1 (300 mL) can cream of potato soup
½ cup whole milk

- Combine all ingredients in saucepan.
- Heat and stir.

Asparagus Chiller

1 (300 mL) can condensed cream of asparagus soup
⅔ cup sour cream
½ cup finely chopped cucumber
2 tablespoons chopped red onion

- Blend soup, sour cream and 1 soup can of water.
- Add cucumber and onion.
- Chill at least 4 hours and serve in chilled bowls.

Yellow Squash Soup

1 kg fresh, yellow squash, thinly sliced
1 onion, chopped
1 (410 mL) can chicken consommé
1 (300 mL) carton sour cream

- In a saucepan simmer squash and onions in the broth until very tender.
- Chill.
- Just before serving, add sour cream and a little salt and pepper.
- Serve chilled.

Red and Green Salad

500 g fresh baby spinach

2 punnets strawberries, halved

$^1/_2$ cup slivered almonds, toasted

Poppy seed dressing made with: 1 cup Italian salad dressing and 1 tablespoon poppy seeds, mixed in

- Tear spinach into smaller pieces and add the strawberries and almonds.
- Refrigerate until ready to serve.
- Toss with poppy seed dressing.

Sesame-Romaine Salad

1 large head romaine or cos lettuce

2 tablespoons sesame seeds, toasted

6 strips bacon, fried, crumbled

$^1/_2$ cup grated Swiss cheese

- Wash and dry lettuce. Tear into bite-size pieces.
- When ready to serve, sprinkle sesame seeds, bacon and cheese over lettuce and toss with a creamy Italian dressing.

Salad Surprise

250 g fresh spinach leaves, washed, stemmed

1 punnet fresh strawberries, stemmed, halved

1 large banana, sliced

$^2/_3$ cup chopped walnuts

- Place all salad ingredients in a large bowl.
- When ready to serve, toss with poppy seed dressing (see Red and Green Salad above).

Strawberry-Spinach Salad

250 g fresh baby spinach leaves, washed, dried

1 small jicama (yam bean), peeled, julienned

1 punnet fresh strawberries, stemmed, halved

$2^1/_2$ cups fresh bean sprouts

- Combine spinach, jicama, strawberries and bean sprouts in a large bowl.
- Toss with poppy seed dressing just before serving.

Poppy seed dressing, see Red and Green Salad.

Mandarin Salad

1 head mignonette lettuce

2 (275 g) cans mandarin oranges, drained

2 avocados, peeled, diced

1 small red onion, sliced

- Combine all ingredients.
- When ready to serve, toss with a poppy seed dressing.

Crunchy Salad

$^1/_4$ cup sesame seeds

$^1/_2$ cup sunflower seeds

$^1/_2$ cup almonds

1 head red leaf lettuce

- Toast the sesame seeds, sunflower seeds and almonds in a 150°C oven for about 15 minutes or until lightly browned.
- Tear lettuce into bite-size pieces and add seed mixture.
- Toss with creamy Italian dressing.

Oriental Spinach Salad

300 g fresh baby spinach leaves

2 (280 g) can bean shoots, drained

8 slices bacon, cooked crisp

2 (190 g) cans water chestnuts, chopped

- Combine spinach and bean shoots.
- When ready to serve, add the crumbled bacon and toss with a vinaigrette salad dressing made from 3 parts olive oil and 1 part red wine vinegar.

Swiss Salad

1 large head cos lettuce

1 bunch fresh green onions with tops, chopped

1 (250 g) packet of shredded Swiss cheese

½ cup toasted sunflower seeds

- Tear the lettuce into bite-size pieces.
- Add onions, cheese, sunflower seeds and toss.
- Serve with a vinaigrette dressing.

Vinaigrette for Swiss Salad

⅔ cup oil

⅓ cup red wine vinegar

1 tablespoon seasoned salt

- Mix all ingredients and refrigerate.

Spinach-Bacon Salad

1 (300 g) packet fresh spinach

2 hardboiled eggs, chopped

8 mushroom caps, sliced

1 (190 g) can water chestnuts, chopped

- Mix all ingredients together and serve with hot bacon dressing.

Hot Bacon Dressing for Spinach Bacon Salad

250 g bacon, chopped

1 cup sugar

1$^{1}/_{3}$ cups white vinegar

5 teaspoons cornflour

- To make dressing, fry the bacon until crisp. Remove bacon to drain and leave bacon drippings in frying pan.
- Add the sugar and vinegar to the frying pan, stirring well. Add one cup water and bring to the boil.
- Mix cornflour with $^{2}/_{3}$ cup water and stir unti dissolved. Pour cornflour mixture into the frying pan with the dressing. Return to the boil; simmer for 5 minutes.
- Remove from heat and toss salad with warm bacon dressing.

Orange-Almond Salad

1 head green coral leaf lettuce

4 slices bacon, fried, crumbled

$^{1}/_{3}$ cup slivered almonds, toasted

1 (310 g) can mandarin oranges, drained, chilled

- Combine all ingredients in a salad bowl.
- When ready to serve toss with a vinaigrette dressing.

Spinach-Orange Salad

300 g fresh baby spinach leaves, stems removed

2 (310 g) cans mandarin oranges, drained

3 radishes, peeled, julienned

1/3 cup slivered almonds, toasted

- In a large bowl, combine spinach, oranges, radishes and almonds.
- Toss with vinaigrette dressing.

Spinach Salad Oriental

300 g fresh baby spinach

2 hardboiled eggs, sliced

1 (280 g) can bean shoots, drained

1 (250 g) can water chestnuts, chopped

- Combine all four ingredients. Top with dressing.

Dressing for Spinach Salad Oriental

3/4 cup olive oil

1/3 cup sugar

1/4 cup tomato sauce (ketchup)

3 tablespoons red wine vinegar

- Combine all ingredients, mixing well.
- You do not need all of this dressing for this salad. Refrigerate remaining salad dressing.

Red Hot Onions

3 large purple onions

2 tablespoons Tabasco

3 tablespoons olive oil

3 tablespoons red wine vinegar

- Slice onions thinly. Pour a cup of boiling water over onions and let stand 1 minute; drain.
- Mix Tabasco, oil and vinegar and pour over onion rings in a shallow bowl with a lid.
- Refrigerate and let stand at least 3 hours.
- Drain to serve.

Good with a barbecue.

Special Spinach Salad

1 (300 g) packet fresh spinach

1 (410 g) can bean shoots, drained

8 slices bacon, cooked crisp

1 (310 g) can water chestnuts, chopped

- Combine spinach and bean shoots.
- When ready to serve add the crumbled bacon and toss with a vinaigrette salad dressing made from 3 parts olive oil and 1 part red wine vinegar.

Red Cabbage Slaw

1 large head red cabbage

2 onions, chopped

½ cup coleslaw dressing

½ cup French dressing

- Slice cabbage and combine with onions.
- Combine dressing and toss with cabbage and onions.
- Refrigerate.

Hawaiian Slaw

$1^1/_2$ level tablespoons unflavoured gelatine

3 cups orange juice, divided

1 (440 g) can crushed pineapple, undrained

2 cups finely shredded cabbage

- Sprinkle gelatine over 1 cup orange juice in a saucepan. Heat until gelatine is dissolved.
- Stir in remaining orange juice and chill until slightly thickened.
- Fold in pineapple and cabbage; mix well.
- Pour into a 20 × 20 cm dish and refrigerate until set.

Devilled Eggs

6 hardboiled eggs

2 tablespoons sweet pickle relish

3 tablespoons mayonnaise

$^1/_2$ teaspoon mustard

- Peel eggs and cut in half lengthwise. Take yolks out and mash with fork.
- Add relish, mayonnaise and mustard to yolks. Place this yolk mixture back into the egg white halves.
- Sprinkle with paprika, if you like.

Broccoli and Pepperoni Salad

250 g bunch broccoli

125 g fresh mushrooms, sliced

170 g Swiss cheese, diced

85 g sliced pepperoni, chopped

- Cut off broccoli florets; combine broccoli, mushrooms, cheese, pepperoni.
- Toss with an Italian dressing.
- Refrigerate at least 8 hours before serving.

Bean and Onion Salad

1 (425 g) can whole green beans

1 (425 g) can yellow beans

$^1/_2$ cup finely chopped red onion

$^1/_4$ cup slivered almonds

- Combine all ingredients and mix with dressing recipe below.

Dressing for Bean and Onion Salad

$^1/_4$ cup oil

1 tablespoon white vinegar

1 teaspoon sugar

2 teaspoons Dijon mustard

- Combine all ingredients adding $^1/_2$ teaspoon salt and $^1/_2$ teaspoon black pepper.
- Pour over bean and onion salad.
- Refrigerate at least 1 hour before serving.

Cashew-Pea Salad

1 (500 g) packet frozen green peas, thawed

$^1/_4$ cup diced celery

1 bunch fresh green onions with tops, chopped

1 cup chopped cashews

- Combine the peas, celery, onions and cashews.
- Toss with $^1/_2$ cup mayonnaise seasoned with $^1/_2$ teaspoon seasoned salt and black pepper.

Marinated Brussel Sprout Medley

500 g packet frozen brussel sprouts
1 cup Italian dressing
1 cup chopped green capsicum
$^{1}/_{2}$ cup chopped onion

- Pierce packet of brussel sprouts and cook in microwave for 7 minutes.
- Mix together the Italian dressing, capsicum and onion.
- Pour over brussel sprouts and marinate for at least 24 hours.
- Drain to serve.

Marinated Brussel Sprouts

500 g fresh brussel sprouts, boiled and drained
$^{1}/_{2}$ cup salad oil
$^{1}/_{4}$ cup white wine vinegar
$^{1}/_{4}$ cup sugar

- Mix all ingredients and marinate overnight.
- Serve cold.

Fusilli Pasta Salad

1 (450 g) packet fusilli or corkscrew pasta
1 (500 g) packet frozen broccoli-cauliflower combination
1 (250 g) packet mozzarella cheese, cut in small chunks
1 (250 g) bottle Thousand Island dressing

- Cook pasta according to packet directions. Drain and cool.
- Cook vegetables in microwave according to packet directions. Drain and cool.
- In a large bowl, combine pasta, vegetables and cheese chunks.
- Toss with dressing. Refrigerate several hours before serving.

Sunshine Salad

2 (420 g) cans corn kernels, drained

2 (400 g) cans peas, drained

1 (420 g) can kidney beans, rinsed, drained

1 (250 mL) bottle Italian dressing

- In a large bowl, combine corn, peas and beans.
- Pour salad dressing over vegetables and chill several hours.

Sour Cream Potato Salad

12 medium red potatoes, unpeeled

1¼ cups mayonnaise

1 cup sour cream

1 cup fresh green onions (shallots) and tops, chopped

- Boil red potatoes until done, about 20 minutes. Slice potatoes.
- Combine mayonnaise, sour cream and 1 teaspoon salt.
- When potatoes are cool toss with sour cream mixture (1 tablespoon horseradish can be added). Add green onion.

Carrot Salad

3 cups finely grated carrots

1 (220 g) can crushed pineapple, drained

4 tablespoons coconut

1 tablespoon sugar

- Combine all ingredients. Toss with ⅓ cup mayonnaise, mixing well.
- Refrigerate.

Cucumber Salad

1 (85 g) packet lime jelly crystals

2 medium cucumbers

1 tablespoon minced onion

$^1/_2$ cup mayonnaise, $^1/_2$ cup sour cream

- Dissolve jelly crystals in $^3/_4$ cup boiling water; mixing well. Bring to room temperature.
- Slice cucumber in half and remove seeds. Grate cucumber and add to cooled jelly crystals along with the onion, mayonnaise and sour cream.
- Pour into a square dish.
- Refrigerate until set.

Chilled Cucumbers

2 cucumbers, peeled, sliced

$^1/_2$ onion, sliced

$^1/_4$ cup vinegar

$^1/_3$ cup sugar

- Place cucumbers and onion in a bowl with a lid.
- Combine vinegar and sugar. Pour over cucumbers and onions.
- Cover and chill for 2 to 3 hours before serving.

Marinated Cucumbers

$^1/_3$ cup vinegar

2 tablespoons sugar

1 teaspoon dried dill

3 cucumbers, peeled, sliced

- Combine the vinegar, sugar, 1 teaspoon salt, dill and about $^1/_4$ teaspoon black pepper. Pour over the cucumbers.
- Refrigerate 1 hour before serving.

You could add onion to the cucumbers if you like.

Stuffed Cucumber Slices

3 cucumbers, peeled

1 (125 g) packet cream cheese, softened

$^1/_4$ cup stuffed green olives, chopped

$^1/_2$ teaspoon seasoned salt

- Halve cucumbers lengthwise and scoop out seeds.
- Beat cream cheese with mixer, until creamy. Add olives and seasoned salt.
- Fill hollows with cream cheese mixture, press halves together and wrap tightly in plastic wrap; chill.
- Cut crosswise in $1^1/_2$ cm slices to serve.

Nutty Grape-Pineapple Salad

500 g seedless green grapes, halved

$^1/_2$ cup chopped pecans

$^2/_3$ cup shredded cheddar cheese

1 (450 g) can pineapple pieces, drained

- Combine grapes, pecans, cheese and pineapple. Fold in about $^1/_2$ cup of mayonnaise.
- Serve on lettuce leaves.

Marinated Onion Rings

1 kg white onions, thinly sliced

1 cup sugar

2 cups white vinegar

$^1/_2$ teaspoon salt

- Cover onions with boiling water and let stand for five minutes. Drain.
- Combine sugar, vinegar and salt; pour over onions.
- Refrigerate.

Broccoli Salad

5 cups cut broccoli, florets (no stems)

1 sweet red capsicum, julienned

1 cup chopped celery

250 g mild cheddar cheese, cubed

- Combine all ingredients and mix well.
- Toss with Italian or your favourite dressing. Refrigerate.

Green Beans with Tomatoes

1 kg frozen, cut green beans

4 tomatoes, chopped

1 bunch green onions, chopped

1 cup Italian salad dressing

- Place beans in a saucepan and cover with water; bring to the boil. Cook uncovered for 8 to 10 minutes or until tender crisp; drain, chill.
- Add the tomatoes, green onions and salad dressing; toss to coat.

Green and White Salad

1 (500 g) packet frozen green peas, thawed, uncooked

1 head cauliflower, cut into bite-size pieces

1 (300 mL) carton sour cream

2 teaspoons lemon pepper

- In a large bowl, combine the peas and cauliflower.
- Combine sour cream and lemon pepper. Toss with the vegetables.
- Refrigerate.

Salad is even better if you add half of a purple onion, chopped.

Colour-Coded Salad

1 (500 g) packet tri-coloured macaroni, cooked, drained

1 red capsicum, julienned

1 cup chopped zucchini

1 cup broccoli florets

- Combine all ingredients.
- Toss with about 1 cup of Caesar salad dressing.
- Refrigerate.

Snicker Salad

6 large delicious apples, unpeeled, chopped

6 (55 g) Snicker candy bars, chopped

½ cup chopped pecans, optional

1 (600 mL) carton thickened cream, whipped

- In a large bowl, combine apples, candy bars and pecans; mixing well.
- Fold in whipped cream.
- Refrigerate.

It is better served the same day.

Cool Apricot Salad

1 (440 g) can crushed pineapple, undrained

2 (85 g) packets apricot jelly crystals

2 cups buttermilk

1 (600 mL) carton thickened cream, whipped

- Bring pineapple and juice to the boil. Add the jelly crystals and stir until well dissolved. Cool completely.
- When mixture begins to thicken, add buttermilk and fold in the whipped cream.
- Pour into a 23 × 33 cm glass or stainless steel baking dish and refrigerate until set.
- Cut into squares and serve.

Pineapple-Ginger Salad

1 (825 g) can pineapple pieces, reserve juice

2 (85 g) packets lime jelly crystals

1 cup ginger ale

¼ teaspoon ground ginger

- Heat ½ cup pineapple juice (if not enough juice, add water to make ½ cup). Pour boiling juice over jelly crystals, mixing well.
- Add ginger ale and ginger. Chill until slightly thickened.
- Fold in pineapple pieces and spoon into a 18 × 28 cm shallow dish.
- Refrigerate.

Salad Berry Dream

1 (175 g) packet blackberry jelly crystals

1 (475 g) can crushed pineapple, juice reserved

1 (475 g) can blueberries, drained

Whipped cream, optional

- Add enough water to the pineapple juice to make 2 cups. Put in saucepan and bring to the boil. Pour hot liquid over the jelly crystals and mix until dissolved.
- Chill until this mixture begins to thicken. Stir in pineapple and blueberries.
- Pour into a 18 × 28 cm dish. Refrigerate.

Topping for Salad Berry Dream

1 (250 g) packet cream cheese, softened

1 (250 g) carton sour cream

½ cup sugar

½ cup chopped pecans

- In mixer beat together the cream cheese, sour cream and sugar. Beat until smooth and fluffy.
- Spoon over congealed salad.
- Sprinkle pecans over congealed salad.
- Refrigerate.

Cherry Crush

1 (175 g) packet cherry jelly crystals

1 (250 g) packet cream cheese, softened

1 (600 g) can cherry pie filling

1 (475 g) can crushed pineapple, undrained

- Dissolve jelly crystals with $^3/_4$ cup of boiling water.
- With electric mixer beat in the cream cheese, beating very slowly at first. Fold in pie filling and crushed pineapple.
- Pour into a 20 × 30 cm casserole dish. Refrigerate.

Cashew Cocktail Salad

2 (85 g) packets lemon jelly crystals

1 litre vanilla ice cream

1 (420 g) can fruit cocktail, drained

$1^1/_4$ cups chopped cashew nuts

- Dissolve jelly crystals in 1 cup boiling water and stir in ice cream. Blend until ice cream is melted.
- Add fruit cocktail and cashew nuts; mix well.
- Pour into a 20 × 28 cm glass dish. Refrigerate overnight.

Luscious Strawberry Salad

2 (85 g) packets strawberry jelly crystals

2 (300 mL) boxes frozen strawberries, thawed

3 bananas, sliced

1 (300 mL) carton sour cream

- Dissolve jelly crystals in 1 cup boiling water, mixing well. Add strawberries and bananas.
- Pour half mixture in a 23 × 33 cm dish, leaving all the bananas in the bottom layer. Chill until firm. Reserve remaining jelly at room temperature.
- Spread sour cream over firm jelly.
- Add remining jelly over sour cream. Refrigerate until firm.

Tropical Mango Salad

2 (440 g) cans mangoes, drained, reserve juice

2 (85 g) packets orange jelly crystals

1 (250 g) packet cream cheese, softened

1 cup whipped cream

- Place all mango slices on a dinner plate and with a knife and fork, cut slices into bite-size pieces. Place $1^1/_2$ cups of the mango juice (if not that much juice, add water to make $1^1/_2$ cups) in a saucepan and bring to boiling point.
- Pour hot juice over jelly crystals in mixer bowl and mix well.
- Add cream cheese and start mixer very slowly. Gradually increase speed until cream cheese is mixed into jelly. Pour in mango pieces.
- Place in refrigerator until it is lightly congealed. Fold in whipped cream. Pour into a 18 × 28 cm dish. Chill for several hours.

Salad Supreme

2 (85 g) packets orange jelly crystals

1 (250 g) packet cream cheese, softened

2 (440 g) cans mangoes, undrained

2 (310 g) cans mandarin oranges, drained

- Place jelly crystals in mixing bowl and pour $^3/_4$ cup boiling water over crystals and mix well. Let partially cool and add cream cheese.
- At a very slow speed at first, beat in the cream cheese until well mixed.
- Fold in mangoes and mandarin oranges. Pour into 8-cup moulds.
- Chill several hours.

Pineapple Salad

1 (825 g) can crushed pineapple, undrained

2 (85 g) packets lemon jelly crystals

1 (250 g) packet cream cheese, softened

1 (300 mL) carton thickened cream, whipped

- Heat pineapple to boiling. Pour over jelly crystals in mixing bowl and stir to dissolve.
- Combine pineapple mixture and cream cheese; whip slowly until well combined.
- Chill until partially set.
- Fold in the whipped cream and pour into an 8-cup mould.

Apple-Pineapple Salad

2 (85 g) packets lemon jelly crystals

1 (440 g) can pineapple pieces, undrained

1 cup diced apples, unpeeled

1 cup chopped pecans

- Dissolve jelly crystals in 1 cup boiling water. Add pineapple and place in refrigerator until slightly thickened.
- Fold in apples and pecans.
- Pour into a solid mould or into a 18 × 28 cm dish. Chill until firm.

Pineapple-Banana Salad

2 (85 g) packets lime jelly crystals

1 (250 g) can crushed pineapple, undrained

½ cup sour cream

1 large banana, sliced

- Dissolve jelly crystals in 1 cup boiling water; mixing well. Stir in pineapple.
- Place in refrigerator until mixture begins to thicken.
- Fold in sour cream and banana and pour into a 20-cm mould. Chill 3 to 4 hours.

A ½ cup chopped pecans could be added.

Glazed Fruit Salad

2 (310 g) cans mandarin oranges, drained

1 (440 g) can pineapple pieces, drained

3 bananas, sliced

1 (500 mL) carton creamy glaze for bananas

- In a large bowl combine fruit and glaze.
- Toss to coat fruit.
- Serve immediately.

Grapes, apples or marshmallows could also be added to this salad.

Lime-Cherry Salad

1 (85 g) packet lime jelly crystals

1 (300 g) bottle maraschino cherries, drained, halved

1 cup diced apples, unpeeled

1 cup chopped pecans

- Dissolve jelly crystals in 1½ cups boiling water; mixing well.
- Add the drained cherries and place in refrigerator until slightly congealed.
- Add apples and pecans and pour into a 18 × 28 cm dish. Chill until firm.

Orange-Pear Salad

1 (400 g) can sliced pears, reserve juice

1 (85 g) packet orange jelly crystals

1 (250 g) packet cream cheese, softened

1 (300 mL) carton thickened cream, whipped

- Drain pears and reserve juice. Boil juice and ½ cup water. Then add jelly crystals and dissolve. Mix thoroughly and refrigerate until partially set.
- Blend pears and cream cheese in blender. Fold in pear mixture and whipped cream into jelly mixture. Blend well.
- Pour into a 18 × 28 cm shallow dish. Refrigerate 4 hours until set.

Applesauce Salad

2 cups applesauce

1 (85 g) packet lime jelly crystals

2 (350 mL) cans lemon lime carbonated drink

1 (250 g) can crushed pineapple, drained

- Heat applesauce in a large saucepan.
- Add jelly crystals to the hot applesauce and stir until dissolved. Add lemon line drink and pineapple.
- Pour into a 20-cm mould. Refrigerate.

Coconut-Orange Salad

1 (85 g) packet orange jelly crystals

$^1/_2$ litre vanilla ice cream, softened

$^1/_2$ cup coconut

1 (300 g) can mandarin segments, drained

- Dissolve jelly crystals in 1 cup boiling water. Let cool slightly. Fold in ice cream, coconut and mandarin segments.
- Pour into a 18 × 28 cm dish and refrigerate.

Coconut Bananas

4 bananas

4 tablespoons lemon juice

1 (300 mL) carton sour cream

$1^1/_4$ cups flaked coconut

- Cut bananas into quarters.
- Place lemon juice, sour cream and coconut in separate bowls.
- Dip bananas into lemon juice, roll in sour cream and then in coconut. Cover thoroughly.
- Place in covered bowl and refrigerate several hours or overnight. Serve as accompaniment to curries.

Grapefruit-Avocado Salad

4 grapefruit, segmented

2 ripe avocados, peeled, sliced

½ cup chopped slivered almonds

Prepared poppy seed dressing

- Combine grapefruit, avocados and almonds.
- Toss with the poppy seed dressing. Serve on a bed of lettuce.

Poppy seed dressing, see Red and Green Salad.

Crunchy Fruit Salad

2 red apples, chopped

⅓ cup sunflower seeds

½ cup green grapes

⅓ cup vanilla yoghurt

- In a bowl, combine the apples, sunflower seeds, grapes and yoghurt. Stir to coat salad. Refrigerate until serving.

Cranberry Mousse

1 (425 g) jar jellied cranberry sauce

1 (250 g) can crushed pineapple, drained

1 (300 mL) carton sour cream

1 tablespoon mayonnaise

- In a saucepan place the cranberry sauce and crushed pineapple. Cook until cranberry sauce is liquid.
- Fold in the sour cream and mayonnaise.
- Pour into moulds or muffin tins and freeze. Serve with cold ham or turkey.

Chicken Caesar Salad

4 boneless, skinless chicken breasts, grilled

1 (125 g) packet cos salad greens

$^1/_2$ cup shredded parmesan cheese

1 cup seasoned croutons

- Cut chicken breasts into strips.
- Combine chicken, salad greens, cheese and croutons in a large bowl.
- When ready to serve, toss with about $^3/_4$ cup Caesar Italian dressing.

Mexican Chicken Salad

3–4 boneless, skinless chicken breasts, cooked, cubed

1 (440 g) can chick peas (garbanzo beans), drained

1 red capsicum, 1 green capsicum, seeded, diced

1 cup chopped celery

- Combine all ingredients and serve with the following dressing.

Dressing for Mexican Chicken Salad

$1^1/_2$ cups sour cream

2 tablespoons chilli sauce

2 teaspoons ground cumin

1 small bunch coriander, finely chopped

- Combine all ingredients for the dressing. Add a little salt and black pepper.
- Pour over chicken salad and toss. Chill before serving.

Tarragon-Chicken Salad

1 cup chopped, toasted pecans

3–4 boneless, skinless chicken breasts, cooked, cubed

1 cup chopped celery

$^{3}/_{4}$ cup peeled chopped cucumbers

- Place pecans in a shallow pan; toast at 150°C for 10 minutes.
- Combine the chicken, celery and cucumbers.

Dressing for Tarragon-Chicken Salad

$^{2}/_{3}$ cup mayonnaise

1 tablespoon lemon juice

2 tablespoons tarragon vinegar

$1^{1}/_{4}$ teaspoons crumbled, dried tarragon

- Mix all dressing ingredients together. When ready to serve toss with the chicken mixture, add pecans.

Apple-Walnut Chicken Salad

3–4 boneless, skinless chicken breasts, cooked, cubed

2 tart green apples, peeled, chopped

$^{1}/_{2}$ cup chopped pitted dates

1 cup finely chopped celery

- Mix all ingredients together.
- Toss with dressing.

Dressing for Apple-Walnut Chicken Salad

½ cup chopped, toasted walnuts

⅓ cup sour cream

⅓ cup mayonnaise

1 tablespoon lemon juice

- Toast walnuts at 150°C for 10 minutes.
- Mix together sour cream, mayonnaise and lemon juice.
- Mix with walnuts.
- Pour over chicken salad and toss. Refrigerate.

Broccoli-Chicken Salad

3–4 boneless, skinless chicken breasts, cooked, cubed

2 cups fresh broccoli florets

1 sweet red capsicum, seeded, chopped

1 cup chopped celery

- Combine chicken, broccoli, capsicum and celery.
- Toss with a honey mustard dressing. Refrigerate.

Black Bean Chicken Salad

3–4 boneless, skinless chicken breasts, cooked, cubed

1 (440 g) can black beans, drained

1 bunch green onions, chopped

1 cup chopped celery

- Blend all ingredients together and toss with the Cumin Dressing on next page.

Cumin Vinaigrette

$^3/_4$ cup virgin olive oil

$^1/_4$ cup lemon juice

2 teaspoons Dijon mustard

2 teaspoons ground cumin

- Combine all ingredients together.
- Toss with black bean and chicken salad. Refrigerate.

Derby Chicken Salad

3–4 boneless, skinless chicken breasts, cooked, cubed

125 g bacon, cooked, crumbled

2 avocados, peeled, diced

2 tomatoes, diced, drained

- Combine all ingredients.
- When ready to serve pour Italian salad dressing over salad and toss. Refrigerate.

Savoury Chicken Salad

4 boneless, skinless chicken breasts, cooked

1 cup chopped celery

1 red capsicum, seeded, chopped

$^2/_3$ cup slivered almonds, toasted

- Slice chicken breasts into long thin strips.
- Combine chicken, celery, capsicum and almonds. Toss and refrigerate.

For dressing use a flavoured mayonnaise ($^1/_2$ cup mayonnaise with 1 tablespoon lemon juice).

Sweet and Sour Pickles

2 (500 g) jars dill and cucumber pickles, sliced, reserve juice

1½ cups sugar

½ cup white vinegar

¾ teaspoon mustard seeds

- Set aside juice and pickle jar. Place pickles in a bowl and cover with sugar. Let soak overnight.
- Place pickles back in jar.
- Heat juice, vinegar and mustard seeds to a boiling point and pour over pickles. Let set overnight.

Good Night Onions

500 g purple onions, sliced

1 cup tarragon vinegar

½ cup sugar

½ teaspoon salt and pepper

- Place onion rings in a large jar.
- Pour in the vinegar, sugar, ½ teaspoon pepper, ½ teaspoon salt and 1 cup water.
- Cover tightly and shake well until the sugar is dissolved. Store in refrigerator overnight before serving.

Cream Cheese Sandwiches

2 (250 g) packets cream cheese, softened

$^{1}/_{4}$ cup chopped black olives

$^{3}/_{4}$ cup finely chopped pecans

Pumpernickel rye bread

- Beat the cream cheese until creamy. Fold in olives and pecans.
- Trim crusts on bread.
- Spread cream cheese on bread.
- Slice sandwich into 3 finger strips.

Luncheon Sandwich

1 loaf thinly sliced, sandwich bread

240 g butter, softened

1 (125 g) jar cheese spread, softened

$^{1}/_{2}$ teaspoon worcestershire sauce

- Trim crust on the bread.
- With mixer, beat together the butter and cheese spread until smooth and creamy, adding worcestershire sauce.
- Spread mixture on three slices of bread making a triple decker sandwich.
- Place fourth slice of bread on top. Cut into finger sandwiches.

These sandwiches can be served cold or warmed at 150°C for 5 to 10 minutes.

Party Sandwiches

500 g bacon, cooked, crumbled

$^{1}/_{2}$ cup ripe olives, coarsely chopped

$^{1}/_{2}$ cup chopped pecans

$1^{1}/_{4}$ cups mayonnaise

- Mix all ingredients together.
- Spread on thin sliced white bread.
- Cut sandwiches into three strips.

Watercress Tea Sandwiches

1 small bunch of watercress

5 hardboiled eggs, peeled

6 tablespoons mayonnaise

1 tablespoon Dijon mustard

- Trim ½ of the watercress stems. Save the rest for garnish.
- In a food processor, coarsely chop the eggs; add mayonnaise, mustard and a little salt. Process until smooth.
- Fold in the chopped watercress and chill.
- Spread mixture onto thinly sliced white bread that has the crust trimmed. Cut into finger sandwiches.

Cream Cheese Tea Sandwiches

1 (250 g) packet cream cheese, softened

250 g bacon, fried and finely chopped

12–14 slices whole wheat bread

1 (350 g) tub bean shoots

- With a mixer, beat the cream cheese until smooth. Add the finely chopped bacon (or you can chop the cream cheese and bacon together in a food processor).
- On 6 to 8 slices of bread, spread the bacon–cream cheese mixture. Add a layer of bean shoots.
- On the other 6 to 8 slices, spread either mayonnaise or butter and place on top of the bean shoots making 6 or 8 sandwiches.
- With a sharp knife remove crust and cut each sandwich into 3 finger shapes. Refrigerate.

Cream Cheese Sandwich Spread

2 (250 g) packets cream cheese, softened

50 g packet dried beef, finely chopped

1 bunch fresh green onions and tops, chopped

½ cup mayonnaise, 1 teaspoon pepper

- Combine all ingredients together until the mixture will spread smoothly.
- Trim crust of whole wheat bread and spread cream cheese mixture on bread.
- Top with another slice of bread and slice into 3 strips or 4 quarters.

Green Chilli Grilled Cheese

4 sliced bread

4 slices cheddar cheese

½ (250 g) jar sliced jalapeno green chillies, chopped

3 tablespoons margarine, softened

- On 2 slices of bread, place a slice of cheese on each slice. Sprinkle with chopped jalapeno chillies.
- Top with the two remaining slices of cheese; then with remaining two slices of bread.
- Butter the outside of the sandwiches.
- In a large frying pan over medium heat brown sandwiches on both sides until golden brown and cheese has melted.

Confetti Sandwiches

1 tablespoon lemon juice

1 (250 g) packet cream cheese, softened

½ cup grated carrots

¼ cup each grated cucumber, purple onion and red capsicum

- Combine lemon juice with cream cheese; adding enough mayonnaise to make cheese into spreading consistency.
- Fold in grated vegetables and spread on bread for sandwiches. Refrigerate.

Hot Bunwiches

8 hamburger buns

8 slices Swiss cheese

8 slices ham, 8 slices turkey

8 slices cheddar or Tasty cheese

- Lay out all 8 buns. On the bottom bun, place the slices of Swiss cheese, ham, turkey and cheddar/Tasty cheese.
- Place the top bun over the Tasty cheese.
- Wrap each bunwich individually in baking paper. Heat in microwave for 10–15 seconds.
- May be frozen and thawed and heated in microwave oven when needed.

Reubens on a Bun

1 (500 g) smoked frankfurts

8 hot dog buns

1 (250 g) can sauerkraut, well drained

Caraway seeds

1 (250 mL) bottle Thousand Island dressing

- Pierce each frankfurt and place into split buns.
- Arrange two tablespoons sauerkraut over each frank. Sprinkle with caraway seeds.
- Place in a 23 × 33 cm shallow pan and drizzle with Thousand Island dressing.
- Place in 160°C oven for 10 minutes until hot dogs are thoroughly heated.

Italian Sausage Sandwiches

1 (500 g) sweet Italian sausage, cooked, casing removed

1 red capsicum, chopped

1 onion, chopped

1$^{2}/_{3}$ cups Italian-style spaghetti sauce

- In a frying pan over medium heat, cook sausage, capsicum and onion until sausage is brown and no longer pink.
- Stir in spaghetti sauce and heat until boiling. Simmer for 5 minutes stirring constantly.
- Pour mixture over split hot dog rolls.

Pizza Burger

500 g lean ground beef

1/2 teaspoon salt

1/2 cup pizza sauce

4 slices mozzarella cheese

- Combine beef, salt and 1/2 pizza sauce.
- Mould into 4 patties and pan fry over medium heat for 5 to 6 minutes on each side.
- Just before burgers are done, top each with a spoonful of pizza sauce and a slice of cheese.
- Serve on a hamburger bun.

Marshmallow Sandwiches

1 jar marshmallow whip

Chunky peanut butter

White bread or whole wheat bread

Vanilla wafers, optional

- On one slice of bread, spread marshmallow cream.
- On a second slice of bread, spread the peanut butter.
- Put the marshmallow and the peanut butter sides together.

Barking Dogs

10 wieners (Vienna frankfurts)

5 slices cheese

10 corn tortillas

Oil

- Slice wieners lengthwise and halfway through.
- Cut each cheese slice in half and place inside each wiener.
- Wrap tortillas around wiener and secure with a toothpick.
- Heat several cms of oil in frying pan. Fry dogs in oil until tortilla is crisp. Serve hot.

Cheese Doggies

Sliced frankfurts

Cheddar cheese slices

Bacon slices

Hot dog buns

- Use 1 bacon slice for each frankfurt. Place bacon on paper towel or paper plate and cover with a paper towel and microwave for 45 seconds or until almost crisp.
- Cut lengthwise pocket in the frankfurt and stuff with a strip of cheese.
- Wrap bacon around the doggie and secure with toothpick.
- Place in split hot dog bun and microwave for about 30 seconds or until the hot dog is warm.

Dog Wrap

8 Vienna frankfurts

8 slices cheese

2 sheets frozen shortcrust pastry, thawed and cut into 4 squares each sheet

- Split frankfurts lengthwise and fill with a folded cheese slice.
- Wrap in pastry, from pointed side and bake at 190°C for about 15 minutes. Serve with mustard.

Hot and Sweet Mustard

125 g dry mustard

1 cup vinegar

3 eggs

1 cup sugar

- Soak dry mustard in vinegar overnight.
- Beat eggs and sugar together; then add to vinegar–mustard mixture.
- In top of double boiler, cook over low heat for about 15 minutes, stirring constantly. Mixture will resemble a custard consistency. Pour immediately into jars. Store in refrigerator. Serve with ham.

Great to keep in the refrigerator for ham sandwiches.

Avocado Butter

2 large avocados, peeled

2 tablespoons lime juice

250 g butter, softened

$^{1}/_{4}$ teaspoon ginger

- Combine all ingredients in electric blender or food processor. Blend until smooth.
- Serve on crackers or make party sandwiches on white or rye bread.

VEGETABLES and SIDE DISHES

Posh Squash

8 medium yellow squash, sliced

$^1/_2$ green capsicum, seeded, chopped

1 small onion, chopped

1 (250 g) box processed cheddar cheese, cubed

- Combine squash, capsicum and onion in a large saucepan and just barely cover with water.
- Cook just until tender – about 10 to 15 minutes.
- Drain and add cheese; stir until cheese is melted and pour into a buttered 2 litre baking dish.
- Bake at 180°C for 15 minutes.

Squash on the Run

5 yellow squash, sliced

2 potatoes, thinly sliced

1 onion, chopped

1 (410 g) can cream of chicken soup

- In a buttered 2 litre casserole dish, layer the squash, potatoes and onion.
- In a saucepan, combine soup and $^1/_2$ can water; heat just enough to mix well. Pour over vegetables.
- Cover and bake at 180°C for 40–45 minutes.

Seasoned Squash and Onion

8 yellow squash, sliced

2 onions, chopped

60 g margarine

1 cup grated mild cheddar cheese

- Cook squash and onion in a small amount of water until tender; drain.
- Add margarine and cheese and toss. Serve hot.

Dilled Zucchini

120 g butter

8 medium zucchini, grated

$1\frac{1}{2}$ tablespoons chopped fresh dill

Salt and pepper

- In a skillet melt the butter and saute the zucchini and dill. Cook on medium heat for 5 minutes or just until tender.

Add salt and pepper and serve hot.

Stuffed Yellow Squash

5 large yellow squash

1 (500 g) packet frozen chopped spinach

1 (250 g) packet cream cheese, cubed

1 packet dry onion soup mix

- Steam squash whole until tender.
- Slit squash lengthwise and remove the seeds with a spoon.
- Cook spinach according to packet directions. Drain well. Add the cream cheese and stir until it melts. Do not let this boil as the heat will be too hot for the cream cheese. Add soup mix, blending well.
- Fill scooped out squash shells with spinach mixture and top with a few sprinkles of cheddar cheese.
- Place on a baking sheet and bake at 160°C for about 15 minutes.

Sunny Yellow Squash

6–8 medium yellow squash

1 (250 g) packet cream cheese, softened, cubed

2 tablespoons margarine

1 teaspoon sugar

- In saucepan, cut up squash, add a little water and boil until tender. Drain.
- Add cream cheese, margarine, sugar and a little salt and pepper.
- Cook over low heat, stirring until cream cheese has melted.

Fried Zucchini

3 large zucchini, grated

5 eggs

1 cup cracker crumbs

½ cup grated parmesan cheese

- Combine the zucchini, eggs and cracker crumbs, mixing well. Add cheese and a little salt and pepper.
- Drop by spoonfuls into a frying pan with a little hot oil. Fry for about 15 minutes. Brown on each side.

Zucchini Patties

1½ cups grated zucchini

1 egg, beaten

2 tablespoons flour

⅓ cup finely chopped onion

- Mix all ingredients together, adding ½ teaspoon seasoned salt.
- Heat a frying pan with about 3 tablespoons oil.
- Drop zucchini mixture by tablespoons onto the frying pan at medium high heat. Turn and brown both sides. Remove and drain on paper towels.

Stir-Fry Zucchini

30 g margarine

6–8 zucchini, grated

1 teaspoon seasoned salt

$^{1}/_{4}$ cup grated parmesan cheese

- Heat margarine in large frying pan and add zucchini. Cook on medium heat about 8 minutes; stir frequently.
- If zucchini gets too dry, add a tablespoon or so of water. Toss with seasoned salt and parmesan cheese. Serve hot.

Zucchini Beau Monde

6–8 medium zucchini, sliced

1 teaspoon beau monde seasoning

1 (300 ml) carton sour cream

$^{1}/_{4}$ cup grated parmesan cheese

- Saute zucchini in 2 tablespoons of margarine. Cook on low for about 5 minutes.
- Stir in seasoning, sour cream and cheese. Heat but do not boil.

Walnut Zucchini

6–8 zucchini, julienned

$^{1}/_{2}$ red capsicum, julienned

60 g margarine

1 cup chopped walnuts

- Saute zucchini and capsicum in margarine until tender, shaking the pan and tossing the zucchini to cook evenly. Pour off any excess margarine.
- Add the chopped walnuts, some salt and pepper. When walnuts are well blended and heated, serve hot.

Mushrooms and Corn

125 g fresh mushrooms, sliced

3 chopped green onions and tops

2 tablespoons margarine

1 (500 g) packet frozen corn kernels

- Place all ingredients in a 2 litre saucepan and cook on medium heat for 5 to 10 minutes. Add salt and pepper to taste.

Italian Corn

1 (500 g) packet frozen whole corn kernels

2 slices bacon, cooked and diced

1 onion, chopped

1 (420 g) can Italian diced tomatoes

- Place all ingredients in a 2 litre pan.
- Cook until most of the liquid in the tomatoes has cooked out. Add a little salt and pepper. Serve hot.

Stuffed Corn

1 (420 g) can creamed style corn

1 (420 g) can corn kernels, drained

120 g margarine, melted

1 (200 g) packet chicken stuffing mix

- Combine all ingredients together plus seasoning packet and $^1/_2$ cup water and mix well.
- Spoon into a buttered 23 × 33 cm baking pan. Bake at 180°C for 30 minutes.

Corn Au Gratin

3 (420 g) cans corn kernels, drained

1 (125 g) can sliced mushrooms, drained

1 (300 mL) can cream of mushroom soup

1 cup shredded cheddar cheese

- Mix all ingredients together in a saucepan and heat slowly until cheese is melted. Serve hot.

Wild West Corn

3 (420 g) can whole corn kernels, drained

3/4 (415 g) can diced tomatoes, garlic and basil

1 (250 g) packet shredded mild cheddar cheese

1 cup cheese cracker crumbs

- In a large bowl, combine the corn, diced tomatoes and cheese; mix well.
- Pour into a buttered 2 litre baking dish.
- Sprinkle cracker crumbs over casserole. Bake uncovered at 180°C for 25 minutes.

Calico Corn

1 (500 g) packet frozen corn kernels

1 capsicum, chopped

1/3 cup chopped celery

1 (300 g) can cream of chicken soup

- Cook corn in microwave according to packet directions; drain well.
- To the corn add the capsicum and celery. Stir in soup; mixing well.
- Cook in microwave for 4–6 minutes or until well heated.

Corn Pudding

1 (250 g) packet corn muffin mix

1 (440 g) can creamed style sweet corn

1/2 cup sour cream

3 eggs, lightly beaten

- Combine all ingredients and pour into a buttered 2 litre baking dish.
- Bake uncovered at 180°C for about 35 minutes.

Corn Maize

60 g margarine, melted

100 g cream cheese, softened

2 (420 g) cans whole corn kernels, drained

1/3 cup salsa

- Mix margarine and cream cheese together. Add corn and salsa sauce.
- Pour into a 1 litre microwave dish.
- Cover and microwave on medium power for 4–6 minutes until heated through.

Hot Corn Bake

3 (420 g) cans whole corn kernels, drained

1 (300 g) can chicken and corn soup

1 cup salsa

1 (250 g) packet shredded cheddar cheese blend, divided

- Combine corn, chicken and corn soup, salsa and $^1/_2$ the cheese and mix well.
- Pour into a buttered 3 litre oven dish and sprinkle remaining cheese on top.
- Bake at 180°C for 20 to 30 minutes.

Baked Beans and Corn

1 (410 g) can ranch-style beans

1 (410 g) can pork and beans

1 (420 g) can corn kernels, drained

1 (420 g) can chilli without beans

- Combine all ingredients. Spoon into a lightly greased 3 litre baking dish.
- Bake at 150°C for 1 hour.

Classic Baked Bean Stand-By

3 (425 g) cans baked beans

$^1/_2$ cup chilli sauce

$^1/_3$ cup packed brown sugar

4 slices bacon, cooked, crumbled

- In a buttered 3 litre ovenproof casserole dish, combine baked beans, chilli sauce and brown sugar.
- Bake at 160°C for 40 minutes.
- When ready to serve, sprinkle bacon on top.

Chilli Baked Beans

2 (425 g) cans ham flavoured baked beans

1 (425 g) can chilli with beans

1/4 cup molasses

1 teaspoon chilli powder

- Pour visible liquid out of can of pork and beans.
- In a 2 litre casserole combine pork and beans, chilli, molasses and chilli powder. Heat until bubbly.

Italian-Grilled Tomatoes

4 medium tomatoes

Salt and pepper

1/2 teaspoon dried oregano

Italian salad dressing

- Core tomatoes and cut in half crosswise.
- Make a shallow crisscross cut on the surface of the tomatoes. Season the cut surface with salt, pepper and oregano; drizzle with salad dressing.
- Grill, cut side up for about 5 minutes or until heated thoroughly.

Tasty Turnips

6 medium turnips

2 teaspoons sugar

1 teaspoon salt

60 g butter (not margarine), melted

- Peel and dice turnips. Boil with sugar and salt until tender. Drain.
- Add butter to turnips and mash. Serve hot.

Broad Beans

1 (500 g) packet frozen baby broad beans

1 cup chopped celery

3 tablespoons margarine

2 teaspoons lemon juice

- Place broad beans, celery, margarine and lemon juice in a 2 litre saucepan and add $^{1}/_{3}$ cup water.
- Cook until vegetables are tender. You may add salt and pepper if you like.

Sesame Peas

1 (250 g) packet frozen green peas

2 tablespoons sesame seeds

1 teaspoon sugar

60 g margarine

- Cook peas as directed on packet; drain.
- In a saucepan, heat remaining ingredients. Pour over peas. Serve hot.

Swiss Cheesy Peas

3 (440 g) cans green peas and onions, drained

1 (300 mL) carton sour cream

225 g Swiss cheese, grated

2 cups crushed corn flakes

- In a large bowl, combine the peas, onions, sour cream, Swiss cheese and salt to taste.
- Spoon into a buttered 3 litre casserole dish. Sprinkle corn flakes over top.
- Bake uncovered at 180°C for 35 minutes.

Parmesan Peas

2 (250 g) packets frozen green peas

3 tablespoons butter

1 tablespoon lemon juice

1/3 cup grated parmesan cheese

- Place frozen peas, butter and lemon juice in a microwave-safe dish, cover and microwave on high for 3 minutes. Rotate dish 1/2 turn and cook 3 minutes more.
- Stand covered 3 minutes then sprinkle with parmesan cheese. Serve hot.

Sauteed Celery with Water Chestnuts

1 bunch celery leaves trimmed sticks, chopped diagonally

1 (225 g) can water chestnuts, drained and chopped

1/4 cup almonds, toasted

60 g margarine, melted

- Boil celery in salted water just until tender crisp. Drain.
- Sauté the water chestnuts and almonds in the melted margarine.
- Toss together the celery and the water chestnuts–almond mixture. Serve hot.

Fried Okra

Small, fresh garden okra

Milk or buttermilk

Cornmeal

Salt and pepper

- Thoroughly wash and drain okra. Trim conical top.
- Toss okra with a little milk or buttermilk (just enough to make the cornmeal stick). Sprinkle cornmeal over okra and toss.
- Heat 2 or 3 tablespoons of oil in frying pan. Fry okra, turning several times until okra is golden brown and crisp.

Carrots and Peas

1 (420 g) can sliced carrots, drained

1 (420 g) can green peas, drained

60 g margarine

$^1/_3$ cup chopped cashew nuts

- In a saucepan, combine carrots, peas, margarine and cashew nuts.
- Heat until the margarine melts; mix well. Serve hot.

Tangy Carrot Coins

2 (420 g) cans sliced carrots

30 g margarine

2 tablespoons brown sugar

1 tablespoon Dijon mustard

- Place all ingredients in a saucepan. Cook and stir over medium heat for about 2 minutes. Serve hot.

Creamy Carrots with Toasted Almonds

2 (420 g) cans sliced carrots

1 (250 g) can cream of celery soup

$^{1}/_{2}$ cup milk

$^{1}/_{3}$ cup chopped almonds, toasted

- In a saucepan, combine carrots, soup and milk. Over medium heat stir to mix and heat throughout.
- Stir almonds in just before serving. Serve hot.

Dilled Baby Carrots

350 g fresh baby carrots

3 chicken stock cubes or 2 teaspoons stock powder

90 g butter

2 teaspoons chopped dill

- Boil carrots in water with dissolved stock cubes until tender (about 8 minutes). Drain.
- Place in a frying pan with melted butter. Cook on low heat for only a few minutes making sure the butter coats all carrots.
- Sprinkle dill over carrots and shake to coat well. Place in serving dish and serve immediately.

Glazed Carrots

1 (500 g) packet frozen baby carrots

$^{1}/_{4}$ cup apple cider

$^{1}/_{4}$ cup apple jelly

$1^{1}/_{2}$ teaspoons Dijon mustard

- In a saucepan place carrots and apple cider and bring to boil. Reduce heat. Cover and simmer about 8 minutes until carrots are tender.
- Remove cover and cook on medium heat until liquid evaporates; stir in jelly and mustard. Cook until jelly melts and the carrots are glazed.

Brown Sugar Carrots

2 (420 g) cans carrots

60 g margarine

3 tablespoons brown sugar

½ teaspoon ground ginger

- Drain carrots but reserve 2 tablespoons liquid.
- Combine the 2 tablespoons liquid with the margarine, brown sugar and ginger. Heat thoroughly.
- Add carrots, stirring gently and cook 3 minutes. Serve hot.

Speedy Cabbage

1 head cabbage, shredded

30 g margarine

3 tablespoons sour cream

½ teaspoon black pepper

- Sauté cabbage in margarine and about 2 tablespoons water until tender (about 3 to 4 minutes) stirring constantly.
- Stir in sour cream and about ½ teaspoon salt, ½ teaspoon sugar and pepper. Serve hot.

Creamy Cabbage Bake

1 head cabbage, shredded

1 (410 g) can cream of celery soup

½ cup milk

1 (250 g) packet shredded cheddar cheese

- Place cabbage in a 2 litre buttered baking dish.
- Pour celery soup diluted with milk over top of cabbage. Bake covered at 160°C for 30 minutes.
- Remove from oven, sprinkle with cheese and bake uncovered another 5 minutes.

Fried Cabbage

1 small head cabbage, finely chopped

1/2 teaspoon salt

3 tablespoons oil

2 tablespoons Italian salad dressing

- Sprinkle cabbage with salt and set aside for 30 minutes.
- Heat oil in frying pan until very hot. Add the cabbage and stir fry about 5 minutes.
- Remove and add Italian dressing.

Cheesy Baked Eggplant

1 eggplant

1/2 cup mayonnaise

2/3 cup seasoned breadcrumbs

1/4 cup grated parmesan cheese

- Peel eggplant and slice 1 cm thick.
- Spread both sides with mayonnaise and dip in mixture of crumbs and cheese. Coat both sides well.
- Place in a single layer in a shallow baking dish. Bake at 200°C for 20 minutes.

Eggplant Casserole

1 large eggplant

1 cup cracker crumbs

1 cup shredded cheddar cheese, divided

1 (300 g) jar tomatoes and green chilli salsa

- Peel and slice eggplant.
- Place in a saucepan and cover with water. Cook 10 minutes or until tender. Drain well on paper towels.
- Mash eggplant. Stir in crackers, 3/4 cup of the cheese and tomato salsa; mix well.
- Spoon eggplant in a 1 litre buttered baking dish. Sprinkle with remaining cheese. Bake at 180°C for about 30 minutes.

Baked Onions

4 large onions, thinly sliced

$1^1/_2$ cups crushed potato chips

1 cup shredded cheddar cheese

1 (300 g) can cream of chicken soup

- In a 23 × 32 cm baking dish alternate layers of onion, potato chips and cheese.
- Spoon soup over the last layer and pour $^1/_4$ cup milk or $^1/_4$ cup water on top. Sprinkle with a little red or black pepper.
- Bake at 150°C for 1 hour.

Cheesy Baked Onions

4 yellow onions, peeled, sliced

120 g margarine

25 Ritz crackers, crushed

$^1/_3$ cup grated parmesan cheese

- Sauté onions in margarine until transparent.
- Spread $^1/_2$ of the onions in a 2 litre buttered casserole dish. Top with $^1/_2$ of the crackers, $^1/_2$ of the cheese. Repeat layers.
- Bake uncovered at 150°C for 30 minutes.

Onion Casserole

5–6 medium mild onions, thinly sliced

3 tablespoons margarine

1 cup milk

4 eggs

- Sauté onions in margarine in covered frying pan for abut 30 minutes. Cool.
- In bowl beat together milk and eggs. Stir in onions and transfer to greased baking dish. Bake at 160°C for 45 to 50 minutes or until light golden.

Easy Onions

6 medium white onions, peeled and cored

6 beef stock cubes

Worcestershire sauce

60 g margarine, melted

- Place each onion in a piece of heavy-duty aluminium foil.
- Place a stock cube in each onion cavity and several drops of worcestershire sauce. Fill cavity up with margarine and wrap tightly in foil. Place on grill and cook 40 to 45 minutes. (Onion can be baked in the oven at 180°C for 30 to 40 minutes.)

Cheesy Onion Casserole

5 sweet onions, sliced

120 g margarine

1 cup shredded cheddar cheese

22 saltine crackers, crushed

- Sauté onions in margarine until soft.
- In a buttered 2 litre casserole dish layer half the onions, half the cheese, half the crackers. Repeat layers.
- Bake at 160°C for 35 minutes.

Spinach To Like

2 (250 g) packets frozen, chopped spinach

1 (300 mL) carton sour cream

$^1/_2$ packet dry onion soup mix

$^2/_3$ cup seasoned fresh breadcrumbs

- Cook spinach according to packet directions; drain well. Add sour cream and onion soup mix to the spinach.
- Pour into a 2 litre casserole. Sprinkle breadcrumbs on top. Bake at 180°C for 35 minutes.

Creamed Spinach

1 (500 g) packet frozen, chopped spinach

200 g cream cheese, softened

3 tablespoons margarine

1 cup fresh breadcrumbs mixed with a tablespoon of melted butter

- In a saucepan, cook spinach, with $^{3}/_{4}$ cup water for 6 minutes; drain well. Add cream cheese and margarine to the spinach; heat until cream cheese and margarine are melted and mixed well with the spinach.
- Pour into a wide heatproof dish. Sprinkle a little salt over spinach; then cover with the buttered breadcrumbs. Place under a hot grill to brown the crumbs.

Baked Tomatoes with Basil

3 large tomatoes

$1^{1}/_{2}$ cups seasoned fresh breadcrumbs

4 tablespoons butter

Dried basil

- Cut tomatoes in half or slice tomatoes in $1^{1}/_{2}$ to 2 cm thick slices and place on baking sheet.
- Sprinkle slices generously with breadcrumbs and top with butter and basil. Bake at 180°C for 10–15 minutes until lightly brown on top.

Herbed Spinach

2 (500 g) packets frozen, chopped spinach

1 (250 g) packet cream cheese, softened

60 g margarine, melted

1 (170 g) packet herb-seasoned stuffing

- Cook spinach as directed on packet. Drain and add the cream cheese and half of the margarine. Season with a little salt and pepper.
- Pour into a buttered casserole dish. Spread the herb stuffing on top and then drizzle with the remaining margarine.
- Bake at 180°C for 25 minutes.

Favourite Spinach

1 (500 g) packet frozen, chopped spinach, thawed, well drained

1 packet dry onion soup mix

1 (300 mL) carton sour cream

$^{2}/_{3}$ cup shredded mild cheddar cheese

- Combine the spinach, onion soup mix and sour cream. Pour into a buttered 2 litre baking dish. Bake at 180°C for 20 minutes.
- Take out of oven and sprinkle cheese over the top and place casserole back in oven for 5 minutes.

Cheezy Peas Please

1 (300 mL) can cream of mushroom soup

170 g garlic cheese

2 (400 g) cans green peas, drained

1 teaspoon paprika

- In a saucepan heat soup and cheese until the cheese has melted. Add peas and paprika. Heat.

Spinach Bake

1 (500 g) packet cream cheese, softened

1 (300 mL) can cream of chicken soup, undiluted

2 (500 g) packets frozen, chopped spinach, thawed, well drained

1 cup crushed Ritz crackers

- In mixing bowl, beat the cream cheese until smooth. Add soup; mix well.
- Stir in spinach. Spoon into a well greased 3 litre baking dish.
- Sprinkle cracker crumbs over top of casserole. Bake uncovered at 150°C for 35 minutes.

Creamed Peas and Potatoes

1 kg small new potatoes, quartered

1 (300 mL) can cream of mushroom soup

$^1/_3$ cup milk

1 (250 g) packet frozen peas with pearl onions

- Cook new potatoes about 25 minutes or until tender.
- Add soup, milk, $^1/_2$ teaspoon black pepper and the peas, stirring occasionally. Heat through and serve.

Seasoned Green Beans

4 slices bacon, chopped

1 medium onion, chopped

2 (400 g) cans green beans, drained

1 teaspoon sugar

- Sauté bacon and onions in a frying pan. Drain.
- Add green beans and sugar and heat thoroughly.

Italian Green Beans

1 (500 g) packet frozen green beans

3 green onions and tops, chopped

3 tablespoons margarine

1 teaspoon mixed Italian herb seasoning

- Place frozen beans and all other ingredients in a 2 litre saucepan and cook over low heat with lid on, until crisp, tender.

Green Beans

500 g fresh green beans

2 tablespoons soy sauce

$^1/_4$ teaspoon ground nutmeg

$^1/_2$ cup toasted sesame seeds

- Cook green beans in boiling water until tender crisp, about 10 minutes, drain.
- Combine the soy sauce, nutmeg and 2 tablespoons margarine. Cook over medium heat for a few minutes.
- Add to green beans and toss lightly.
- Add sesame seeds, toss again.

Crunchy Green Beans

3 (400 g) cans whole green beans

2 (300 mL) cans cream of mushroom soup

2 (227 g) cans water chestnuts, chopped

1 onion cut into rings and fried

- Combine green beans, mushroom soup, water chestnuts, $^1/_2$ teaspoon of salt and a little pepper.
- Pour into a 2 litre casserole. Bake covered at 180°C for 30 minutes.
- Remove casserole from oven and sprinkle onion rings over top and bake 10 minutes longer.

Green Beans and Almonds

1 kg packet frozen green beans

30 g margarine

2 (227 g) cans water chestnuts, chopped

$^1/_2$ cup slivered almonds, toasted

- Cook beans according to the packet directions.
- Drain, add margarine and heat just until margarine melts. Fold in water chestnuts.
- Place in serving dish and sprinkle almonds over the top.

Souper Cauliflower

1 (500 g) packet frozen cauliflower, cooked, drained

1 (410 g) can cream of celery soup

$^{1}/_{4}$ cup milk

1 cup shredded cheddar cheese

- Place cauliflower in a 2 litre greased baking dish.
- In a saucepan, combine soup, milk and cheese; heat just enough to mix well. Pour over cauliflower.
- Bake at 180°C for 15 minutes.

Savoury Cauliflower

1 head cauliflower

1 (35 g) envelope hollandaise sauce mix

Fresh parsley to garnish

Lemon slices to garnish, optional

- Cut cauliflower into small florets. Cook in salted water until barely tender. Do not overcook.
- Mix sauce as directed on packet.
- Drain cauliflower, top with sauce and a sprinkling of parsley.

Cauliflower Whiz

1 head cauliflower

1 (125 g) jar processed cheese spread, melted

- Place cauliflower on a microwaveable plate. Cover with plastic wrap leaving a 2-cm vent opening. For each 500 g of cauliflower, microwave on high for 7 minutes.
- When done remove plastic wrap and pour melted processed cheese spread over top.

Best Cauliflower

1 (500 g) packet frozen cauliflower

1 (300 mL) carton sour cream

$1^{1}/_{2}$ cups grated cheddar cheese

4 teaspoons sesame seeds, toasted

- Cook cauliflower as directed on packet.
- Drain and place half of cauliflower in a 2 litre baking dish. Sprinkle a little salt and pepper on cauliflower. Spread one half of the sour cream and one half of the cheese. Top with 2 teaspoons sesame seed. Repeat layers.
- Bake at 180°C for about 15 to 20 minutes.

Broccoli with Creamed Corn and Almonds

1 (500 g) packet frozen broccoli florets

1 (250 g) can cream style sweet corn

100 g cream cheese

1 tablespoon lemon juice

$^{1}/_{3}$ cup slivered almonds, toasted

- Cook broccoli as directed on packet.
- Combine in saucepan the sweet corn, cream cheese and lemon juice. Heat slowly until cream cheese is melted.
- When ready to serve pour over cooked broccoli and sprinkle almonds over top of sauce.

Lemon Broccoli

1 kg packet frozen broccoli florets

60 g butter

1 tablespoon lemon juice

$^{1}/_{2}$ teaspoon seasoning salt

- Cook broccoli according to packet directions; drain.
- Melt butter and stir in lemon juice and seasoned salt.
- Pour over broccoli and toss to coat.

Crunchy Broccoli

1 (500 g) packet frozen broccoli florets

1 (200 g) can sliced water chestnuts, drained, chopped

120 g margarine, melted

1 packet dry onion soup mix

- Place broccoli in a microwave dish; cover and microwave 5 minutes. Turn dish and cook another 4 minutes.
- Add the water chestnuts. Combine the melted margarine and soup mix, blending well. Toss with the cooked broccoli.

Cheddar-Broccoli Bake

1 (40 g) packet cheese sauce prepared to packet directions

½ cup milk

1 (500 g) bag frozen broccoli florets, cooked

Fried onion rings

- In a 2 litre casserole, mix sauce, milk and broccoli.
- Bake at 180°C for 25 minutes.
- Stir. Sprinkle onions over broccoli mixture.
- Bake 5 more minutes.

Broccoli Stuffed Tomatoes

4 medium tomatoes

1 (500 g) packet frozen, chopped broccoli

1 (170 g) roll garlic cheese, softened

½ teaspoon garlic salt

- Cut tops off tomatoes and scoop out pulp.
- Cook broccoli according to packet instruction; drain well.
- Combine broccoli, cheese and garlic salt. Heat just until cheese is melted. Stuff broccoli mixture into tomatoes and place on baking sheet.
- Bake at 190°C for about 10 minutes.

Asparagus Caesar

3 (340 g) cans asparagus spears, drained

60 g margarine, melted

3 tablespoons lemon juice

1/2 cup grated parmesan cheese

- Place asparagus in a 2 litre baking dish. Drizzle on margarine and lemon juice. Sprinkle with cheese (and a little paprika if you like).
- Bake at 200°C for 15 to 20 minutes.

Almond Asparagus

1/3 cup margarine

500–750 g fresh asparagus

2/3 cup slivered almonds

1 tablespoon lemon juice

- Melt margarine in frying pan, add the asparagus and almonds. Sauté 3 to 4 minutes.
- Cover and steam about 2 minutes or until tender crisp.
- Sprinkle lemon and a little salt and pepper over asparagus. Serve hot.

Sesame Asparagus

6 fresh asparagus spears, trimmed

1 tablespoon margarine or butter

1 teaspoon lemon juice

1 teaspoon sesame seeds

- Place asparagus in a frying pan. Sprinkle with salt if desired. Add 1/4 cup water; bring to the boil. Reduce heat. Cover and simmer about 4 minutes. Drain the asparagus and place on a platter.
- Melt the butter and add lemon juice and sesame seeds; drizzle over the asparagus.

Asparagus Bake

3 (425 g) cans asparagus cuts, drained, reserve liquid

3 hardboiled eggs, chopped

½ cup chopped pecans

1 (300 mL) can cream of asparagus soup

- Arrange asparagus in buttered 2 litre baking dish.
- Top with half the eggs and pecans.
- Heat asparagus soup, adding half the reserved liquid from the asparagus.
- Spoon over remaining eggs and pecans. Bake covered at 180°C for 25 minutes.

Vegetable Medley

1 (500 g) packet frozen broccoli, cauliflower and carrots

1 (500 g) packet frozen corn

2 (35 g) packets cheese sauce mix

½ cup milk

- Combine broccoli mixture and corn in a 2 litre greased baking dish.
- Prepare cheese sauce mix to packet directions, adding the ½ cup of extra milk.
- Pour over vegetables.
- Cover and bake at 180°C for about 30 minutes.

Roasted Vegetables

750 g assorted fresh vegetables such as squash, carrots, red capsicum, zucchini, cauliflower or broccoli

1 (225 g) can water chestnuts, drained

1 packet onion soup mix

30 g margarine, melted

- Cut all vegetables in uniform 5-cm pieces and place in a greased 2 litre casserole dish with water chestnuts.
- Combine melted margarine and soup mix and drizzle over vegetables, stirring well.
- Cover and bake vegetables at 200°C for 20 to 25 minutes or until tender, stirring once.

Buttered Vegetables

120 g butter

2 yellow squash, sliced

1 (500 g) packet frozen broccoli, thawed

1 (250 g) packet frozen corn kernels, thawed

- Melt butter in large frying pan and add all vegetables.
- Sauté vegetabes for about 10 to 15 minutes or until tender-crisp. Add a little salt if you like. Serve warm.

Creamy Vegetable Casserole

1 (500 g) packet frozen broccoli, carrots and cauliflower

1 (300 g) can cream of mushroom soup, undiluted

1 (250 g) packet cream cheese

1 cup seasoned croutons

- Cook vegetables according to packet directions; drain and place in large bowl.
- In a saucepan, place the soup and cream cheese; heat just enough to mix easily.
- Pour into the vegetable mixture, mixing well.
- Pour into a 2 litre casserole. Sprinkle with croutons. Bake uncovered at 200°C for 25 minutes or until bubbly.

Veggies to Love

1 (500 g) packet frozen broccoli, cauliflower and carrot combination

1 (420 g) can cream of celery soup

$^{1}/_{3}$ cup milk

1 large onion cut into rings and fried

- Cook vegetables according to packet directions. Add soup and milk, mixing well.
- Pour into a buttered 2 litre casserole dish and sprinkle fried onions over top.
- Bake at 180°C for about 30 minutes or until bubbly.

Potatoes Supreme

1 (1 kg) bag frozen hash brown potatoes, thawed

1 onion, chopped

2 (300 g) cans cream of chicken soup

1 (300 mL) carton sour cream

- In a 23 × 33 cm baking dish, combine potatoes, onion, soup and sour cream.
- Bake covered at 180°C for 1 hour.

This recipe is also good with $^{1}/_{2}$ cup parmesan or cheddar cheese sprinkled on top about the last 5 minutes of baking.

Potatoes with a Zip

1 (750 g) bag frozen hash brown potatoes

1 (500 g) box processed cheddar cheese, cubed

2 cups mayonnaise

1 (250 g) jar jalapeno chilli slices, drained and chopped

- In a large bowl, combine hash browns, cheese, mayonnaise and chillies.
- Spoon into a buttered 23 × 33 cm baking dish. Cover and bake at 160°C for 1 hour.
- Stir twice during baking to prevent burning.

Creamy Cheesy Potatoes

1 (750 g) bag frozen hash brown potatoes

1 (500 g) box processed cheddar cheese, cubed

1 (300 mL) can cream of chicken soup

1 (300 mL) carton sour cream

- In a large bowl, combine hash browns, cheese, soup and sour cream. (You may want to add $^1/_2$ teaspoon salt.)
- Spoon into a buttered 23 × 33 cm baking dish. Cover and bake at 160°C for 1 hour.
- Stir twice during baking to prevent burning.

Creamy Potato Bake

6–8 jacket potatoes, baked

1 (300 mL) carton sour cream

1 (250 g) packet cream cheese, softened

$1^1/_2$ cup shredded cheddar cheese

- Cut potatoes in half lengthwise. Scoop out potatoes leaving a thin wall. Place soft potato in mixing bowl.
- Add salt to taste, sour cream and cream cheese and whip until mixed well. Spoon mashed potatoes back into potato skins; place in a hot oven until potatoes have reheated. Sprinkle cheddar cheese on top of potatoes.

Baked Potato Toppers

1 cup grated cheddar cheese

$^1/_2$ cup sour cream

$^1/_4$ cup margarine, softened

4 tablespoons chopped green onion

- Mix all ingredients and serve on baked potato.

Golden Potato Casserole

1 (500 g) bag frozen hash brown potatoes, thawed

1 (250 mL) carton sour cream

1 (250 g) packet shredded cheddar cheese

1 bunch fresh green onions with tops, chopped

- Combine potatoes, sour cream, cheese and onion in a large bowl and thoroughly mix.
- Pour into a 23 × 33 cm buttered casserole dish. Sprinkle a little paprika on top.
- Cover and bake at 160°C for 55 minutes.

Loaded Baked Potatoes

6 medium to large potatoes

250 g sliced pepperoni

1 (500 g) box processed cheddar cheese, cubed

1 (300 g) jar taco sauce

- Wrap potatoes in foil and bake at 190°C for 1 hour or until done.
- Sauté the pepperoni in a pan. Add the cheese and heat on low until cheese melts. Stir in the taco sauce and heat.
- Halve the potatoes and pour over the pepperoni mixture.

Vegetable Stuffed Potatoes

1 (35 g) packet cheese sauce mix

1 (500 g) bag frozen mixed vegetables, cooked, drained

8 large potatoes, baked in jackets

Black pepper

- In saucepan, prepare cheese sauce to packet directions. Add vegetables and heat.
- Cut a lengthwise slice in the top of each potato.
- Slightly mash the pulp in each potato.
- Spoon sauce mixture onto each potato. Sprinkle with black pepper.

Broccoli Potatoes

5 baking potatoes

Margarine

1 (225 g) packet frozen broccoli and cheese sauce

Paprika to garnish, optional

- Put the potatoes in a 200°C oven for 1 hour. (Potatoes are thoroughly cooked when found to be soft after piercing with a skewer.)
- Just before serving, slit each potato lengthwise.
- Fluff potato up with a fork, adding margarine.
- Heat broccoli and cheese sauce in saucepan and pour over each potato.

Oven-Roasted Potatoes

1 kg potatoes, unpeeled

1 envelope dry onion soup mix

$^{1}/_{3}$ cup oil

$^{1}/_{2}$ teaspoon black pepper

- Wash potatoes and cut into medium-size chunks or wedges.
- In a large plastic bag, add all ingredients. Shake until potatoes are evenly coated.
- Empty coated potatoes into a greased 23 × 33 cm baking pan.
- Bake uncovered at 220°C, stirring twice, 40 minutes or until golden brown. Serves 8.

Philly Potatoes

$4^{1}/_{2}$ cups instant mashed potatoes, prepared hot

2 tablespoons freeze-dried chives

1 (250 g) packet cream cheese, softened

1 egg lightly beaten

- Mix all ingredients, blending well.
- Place in a greased 3 litre casserole dish.
- Bake covered at 180°C for 30 minutes.
- Uncover and bake for 15 minutes more.

Company Potatoes

5 potatoes, peeled and sliced

2 (300 mL) cartons cream

2 tablespoons Dijon mustard

$^1/_3$ cup grated parmesan cheese

- In a greased 23 × 33 cm baking dish, layer potatoes and add a little salt and pepper.
- In a saucepan, combine the cream, mustard, 2 tablespoons margarine and a little garlic powder; heat to boiling. Pour over potatoes.
- Cover and bake at 180°C for 1 hour.
- Uncover and top with parmesan cheese. Bake 10 minutes longer or until potatoes are tender.

Cheddar Potatoes

1 (35 g) packet cheese sauce mix, prepared to packet directions

$^1/_3$ cup sour cream

2 fresh green onions, chopped

3 cups instant seasoned mashed potatoes, prepared

- In a saucepan, heat soup; add sour cream, onion and little black pepper.
- Stir in potatoes until well blended.
- Pour into a buttered 2 litre casserole.
- Cook at 180°C for about 25 minutes.

Peppered Mashed Potatoes

4 cups instant, unsalted mashed potatoes, prepared

2 teaspoons lemon pepper

60 g margarine

$^{1}/_{2}$ cup sour cream

- Combine all ingredients in saucepan.
- Heat on low until potatoes are thoroughly heated, stirring occasionally.

Potato Puff

3 eggs, separated

2 cups instant mashed potatoes, prepared hot

$^{1}/_{2}$ cup sour cream

2 teaspoons dried parsley

- Beat egg whites until stiff but still moist. Set aside.
- Beat yolks into potato mixture.
- Fold in the beaten egg whites, sour cream, parsley, 1 teaspoon seasoned salt and $^{1}/_{2}$ teaspoon white pepper.
- Pour into a buttered 2 litre casserole. Bake uncovered at 180°C for 45 minutes.

Cheesy Potatoes

10–12 new potatoes

1 (300 mL) carton sour cream

60 g margarine, melted

1 (500 g) box processed cheddar cheese, sliced

- Rinse and scrub potatoes well but do not peel. Cut into $^1/_2$-cm slices and place in a large saucepan; cover with water. Cook about 25 minutes until slightly tender. Drain.
- Place half of potatoes in a 23 × 33 cm baking dish. Sprinkle with salt and pepper.
- Spread half of sour cream and half of the melted margarine over top of potatoes. Put half the sliced cheese on top.
- Repeat layer. Bake at 200°C for about 20 minutes or until bubbly.

Baked New Potatoes

500 g new potatoes, unpeeled

1 clove garlic, finely chopped

1 large onion coarsely chopped

120 g butter or margarine

- Par-boil new potatoes. Drain and quarter.
- In large frying pan, sauté onion and garlic with butter until onions start to become translucent. Add potatoes. Toss to coat.
- Place in large casserole dish. Add 1 teaspoon seasoned salt.
- Bake at 180°C, basting occasionally, for 25 to 30 minutes until potatoes are fork tender.

Barbecued New Potatoes

500 g new potatoes

3 tablespoons orange marmalade

1 teaspoon brown sugar

2 tablespoons melted butter or margarine

- Cook new potatoes covered in boiling water until crisp-tender.
- Drain and cut in half. Thread on skewers.
- Combine next 3 ingredients and brush mixture over potatoes.
- Barbecue over medium hot coals until potatoes are browned, about 5 minutes each side. Salt and pepper to taste. Baste frequently. Can be baked at 200°C for 20 minutes.

Mashed Red Potatoes

1½ kg pontiac potatoes, quartered, unpeeled

⅓ cup whole milk

80 g margarine

¼ teaspoon white pepper

- Place potatoes in a large saucepan and cover with water; adding 1 teaspoon salt. Cover and bring to the boil.
- Reduce heat; cook for 25 minutes or until very tender.
- Drain potatoes well and place in a large mixing bowl. Add the milk, butter, pepper and a little salt.
- Beat until potatoes are light and fluffy.

Potato Souffle

$2^2/_3$ cups instant mashed potatoes

2 eggs, beaten

1 cup shredded cheddar cheese

French-fried onion rings

- Prepare mashed potato mix according to packet directions.
- Add eggs, cheese and stir until blended.
- Spoon mixture into a lightly greased 2 litre dish. Sprinkle with onion rings.
- Bake uncovered at 160°C for 25 minutes.

Potato Pancakes

$1^1/_2$ kg white potatoes, peeled, grated

1 onion, finely minced

3 eggs, beaten

$^1/_2$ cup seasoned dry breadcrumbs

- In a large bowl, combine the potatoes, onions, eggs, a little salt and pepper and breadcrumbs and mix well.
- In a frying pan, drop by spoonfuls in hot oil and brown on both sides.

Ham-Baked Potatoes

4 potatoes, well scrubbed, in their jackets

1 cup diced, cooked ham

1 (300 g) can cream of mushroom soup

1 cup shredded cheddar cheese

- Prick each potato with a fork in 3 places. Place around edge of a dinner plate and microwave on high for 12–14 minutes. Cover plate and stand 5 minutes.
- Halve the potatoes, fluff up centres with a fork and rearrange onto plate. Top each half with ham.
- In saucepan, heat the soup with $^1/_4$ cup water, heating until spreadable. Spoon soup over potatoes and top with cheese.
- Microwave on high for 4 minutes or until hot.

Broccoli-Topped Potatoes

4 potatoes, well scrubbed

1 cup diced, cooked ham

1 (300 g) can cream of broccoli soup

$^{1}/_{2}$ cup shredded cheddar cheese

- Prick each potato with a fork in 3 places. Place around edge of a dinner plate and microwave on high for 12–14 minutes. Cover plate and stand 5 minutes.
- Halve the potatoes, fluff up centres with a fork and rearrange onto plate. Top each half with ham.
- Stir the soup in the can until smooth. Spoon soup over potatoes and top with cheese.
- Microwave on high for 4 minutes.

Whipped Sweet Potatoes

1 kg kumera sweet potatoes, peeled, boiled then mashed

60 g margarine, melted

$^{1}/_{4}$ cup orange juice

1 cup miniature marshmallows

- Combine sweet potatoes, margarine, orange juice and $^{1}/_{2}$ teaspoon salt in mixing bowl.
- Beat until fluffy. Fold in marshmallows.
- Spoon into a buttered 2 litre casserole.
- Bake uncovered at 180°C for 25 minutes.

You might sprinkle additional marshmallows and grill until lightly browned.

Sweet Potato Casserole

2 kg kumera sweet potatoes, peeled, par-boiled and sliced

$^{1}/_{2}$ cup chopped pecans

$1^{1}/_{2}$ cups packed light brown sugar

120 g margarine

- Place sweet potatoes into a 2 litre casserole dish. Sprinkle pecans over sweet potatoes.
- Mix brown sugar and margarine with just enough water to make it pourable.
- Bring to the boil and pour syrup over sweet potatoes.
- Bake at 180°C for about 30 minutes until the potatoes are browned.

Tasty Rice Bake

$1^{1}/_{2}$ cups uncooked rice

120 g margarine, melted

1 (300 mL) can French onion soup

1 (225 g) can sliced water chestnuts

- Combine rice, margarine, soup, water chestnuts and $1^{1}/_{4}$ cups water.
- Pour into a buttered 2 litre baking dish. Bake covered at 180°C for 1 hour.

Baked Rice

2 cups uncooked rice

120 g margarine, melted

1 (410 g) can cream of celery soup

1 (300 g) can cream of onion soup

- Combine the rice, margarine, soups and 1 cup water.
- Pour into a buttered 3 litre casserole dish.
- Bake at 180°C covered for 1 hour.

Broccoli and Wild Rice

2 (500 g) packets frozen, chopped broccoli

1 (200 g) box long grain and wild rice

1 (250 g) jar cheddar cheese spread

1 (300 g) can cream of chicken soup

- Cook broccoli and rice according to packet directions.
- Combine all ingredients and pour into a buttered 2 litre casserole dish.
- Bake at 180°C for 25 to 30 minutes or until bubbly.

Tasty Rice

60 g margarine

1 cup raw white rice

1 (500 mL) carton beef stock

¼ cup parmesan cheese

- Melt margarine in a 3 litre casserole dish.
- Add the rice and pour the beef stock over rice.
- Sprinkle with parmesan cheese.
- Cover and bake at 180°C for 45 minutes.

Tasty Rice (2)

1 cup long grain rice

1 (40 g) French onion soup mix

2 cups boiling water

2 tablespoons butter

- Combine all ingredients in a 2 litre microwave-safe casserole dish.
- Cover with plastic wrap, leaving a small vent.
- Microwave on high for 10 to 12 minutes (depending on wattage of oven). Stand covered for 2 minutes before serving.

Spanish Rice

85 g margarine, melted

1 onion, chopped

2 cups cooked rice

1 (300 g) jar tomatoes and green chilli salsa

- In large bowl, combine margarine, onion, rice, tomato salsa, 1/4 cup of water and salt to taste.
- Spoon mixture into a buttered 3 litre casserole dish.
- Cover and and microwave for 8 minutes, stirring after 4 minutes.

Mushroom Rice

1 (180 g) packet chicken rice-a-riso

1 (125 g) can sliced mushrooms, drained

1/3 cup slivered almonds

1 (300 mL) carton sour cream

- Prepare rice as directed on packet.
- Fold in mushrooms, almonds and sour cream. Place over low heat to heat through. Or re-heat in microwave-safe bowl in microwave.

Dinner Rice

2 cups cooked white rice

1 onion, chopped

60 g margarine, melted

1 (250 g) packet shredded cheddar cheese

- Combine all ingredients and mix well.
- Spoon mixture into a buttered 2 litre casserole dish.
- Microwave at 70% power for 6–8 minutes until heated through and cheese is melted.

Rice 'N Beans

4 cups cooked rice

1 (425 g) can pinto beans, undrained

1 cup shredded cheddar cheese

3 tablespoons margarine, melted

- Mix all ingredients together in a saucepan.
- Cook over low heat until cheese is melted. Serve hot.

Easy Rice

1 onion, finely chopped

2 tablespoons margarine

1 cup raw white rice

2 (400 g) cans chicken broth

- Sauté onion in the margarine until transparent.
- In a 2 litre casserole dish combine the onion, rice and broth. Cover and bake at 180°C for 55 minutes.

Chilli-Rice Bake

1 cup instant rice

500 mL sour cream

1 (250 g) jar jalapeno chilli, drained and chopped

1 (250 g) packet shredded mild cheddar cheese

- Cook rice according to directions.
- Add remaining ingredients plus $^1/_2$ teaspoon salt.
- Place in a buttered casserole dish.
- Bake covered at 160°C for 15 to 20 minutes until thoroughly heated.

Spinach Fettuccine

1 (170 g) can tomato paste

1 (140 g) can evaporated milk

120 g margarine or butter

1 (340 g) packet spinach fettuccine

- In a saucepan, combine the tomato paste, milk and heat until margarine is melted.
- Season with a little salt and pepper.
- Cook fettuccine according to directions on packet. Serve sauce over fettuccine.

Creamy Fettuccine

1 (250 g) packet fettuccine

500 g Italian sausage

1 (300 g) can cream of mushroom soup

1 (600 mL) carton sour cream

- Cook fettuccine and drain.
- Cut up sausage in to 2 cm pieces and brown over medium heat cooking for about 8 minutes. Drain.
- Mix all ingredients together and place on a 2 litre greased baking dish or casserole.
- Bake at 160°C for 30 minutes.

Creamy Pasta

1 (250 g) jar roasted red peppers, drained

1 (400 g) can chicken broth

1 (125 g) packet cream cheese

Cooked pasta for serving

- Combine red peppers and broth in a blender, mixing well.
- Pour into a saucepan. Heat to boiling.
- Turn heat down and whisk in cream cheese. Serve over your favourite pasta.

Special Macaroni and Cheese

1 (250 g) packet small macaroni shells

1 (400 g) can diced tomatoes

1 (250 g) box processed cheddar cheese, cubed

3 tablespoons margarine, melted

- Cook shells according to packet directions; drain.
- In a large bowl, combine shells, tomatoes, cheese cubes and margarine.
- Pour into a 2 litre buttered baking dish.
- Bake covered at 180°C for 35 minutes.

Macaroni and Cheese

1 cup uncooked macaroni

1½ cups small curd cottage cheese

1½ cups shredded cheddar cheese

4 tablespoons grated parmesan cheese

- Cook macaroni according to packet directions; drain.
- Combine cottage, cheddar and parmesan cheeses. Combine macaroni with the cheese mixture.
- Spoon into a greased 2 litre baking dish.
- Bake covered at 180°C for 35 minutes.

Carnival Couscous

1 cup couscous

1 chicken stock cube, crumbled

60 g margarine

1 red capsicum, 1 yellow squash, and 1/4 of a head of broccoli, finely chopped

- Cook couscous with stock cube as packet directions, leaving out the butter.
- With margarine in saucepan, sauté the capsicum, squash and broccoli, cooking about 10 minutes or until vegetables are almost tender.
- Combine couscous and vegetables. Serve hot.

MAIN DISHES

Bacon-Wrapped Chicken

6 boneless, skinless chicken breast halves

1 (250 g) tub whipped cream cheese with onion and chives

Margarine

6 bacon strips

- Flatten chicken to 1 cm thickness. Spread 3 tablespoons cream cheese over each.
- Dot with margarine and a little salt.
- Roll up. Wrap each with a bacon strip.
- Place seam-side down in a greased 23 × 33 cm baking dish.
- Bake uncovered at 190°C for 40–45 minutes or until juices run clear. To brown, grill 15 cm from heat for about 3 minutes or until bacon is crisp.

Saucy Chicken

5–6 boneless, skinless chicken breasts

2 cups thick and chunky salsa

1/3 cup packed light brown sugar

1 1/2 tablespoons Dijon-style mustard

- Place chicken breasts in a greased 23 × 33 cm baking dish.
- Combine salsa, sugar and mustard and pour over chicken.
- Cover and bake at 180°C for 45 minutes. Serve over rice.

Golden Chicken

6 boneless, skinless chicken breasts

60 g margarine

1 (300 g) can cream of mushroom soup

1/2 cup sliced almonds

- Place chicken breasts in a greased 23 × 33 cm baking dish.
- In a saucepan, combine margarine, soup, almonds and 1/4 cup water. Heat and mix just until margarine is melted.
- Pour mixture over chicken.
- Cover and bake at 180°C for 1 hour.

Chicken Crunch

4–6 boneless, skinless chicken breasts

$^1/_2$ cup Italian salad dressing

$^1/_2$ cup sour cream

$2^1/_2$ cups corn flakes, crushed

- Place chicken in a zip-top plastic bag; add salad dressing and sour cream. Seal, refrigerate 1 hour.
- Remove chicken from marinade, discarding marinade.
- Dredge chicken in corn flakes; place in a 23 × 33 cm non-stick and oil sprayed baking dish.
- Bake uncovered at 190°C for 45 minutes.

Chilli Pepper Chicken

5 boneless, skinless chicken breasts

$^1/_2$ (35 g) envelope chilli seasoning mix

$^1/_2$ (250 g) jar jalapeno chillies, drained and chopped

Chunky salsa

- Dredge chicken in coating mixture and place in a greased 23 × 33 cm baking dish.
- Bake at 190°C for 25 minutes.
- Remove from oven and spread jalapeno chillies over the 5 chicken breasts and return to oven for 5 minutes. Serve with the salsa over each chicken breast.

Catalina Chicken

6–8 boneless, skinless chicken breast halves

1 (250 g) bottle Thousand Island dressing

1 teaspoon black pepper

$1^1/_2$ cups crushed cracker crumbs

- Marinate chicken breasts in dressing for 3–4 hours, then discard marinade.
- Combine pepper and cracker crumbs.
- Dip each chicken breast in crumbs and place in a large, greased baking dish.
- Bake uncovered at 180°C for 1 hour.

Cola Chicken

4–6 boneless, skinless chicken breasts

1 cup ketchup

1 cup cola

2 tablespoons worcestershire sauce

- Place chicken in a 23 × 33 cm casserole dish. Sprinkle with salt and pepper.
- Mix ketchup, cola and worcestershire sauce and pour over chicken.
- Cover and bake at 180°C for 50 minutes.

Asparagus Chicken

1 packet hollandaise sauce mix

2 large boneless chicken breasts, cut into strips

1 tablespoon lemon juice

1 (420 g) can asparagus spears

- Prepare hollandaise sauce according to directions on packet.
- In a large frying pan with a little oil, cook chicken strips for 12 to 15 minutes or until brown, stirring occasionally.
- Add hollandaise sauce and lemon juice.
- Cover and cook another 10 minutes, stirring occasionally. Serve over hot cooked noodles topped with the heated asparagus spears.

Wine and Chicken

6–8 boneless skinless chicken breasts

1 (300 g) can cream of mushroom soup

1 (300 g) can cream of chicken soup

1 cup white wine

- In a frying pan, brown chicken in a little bit of oil. Place in a 23 × 33 cm baking dish.
- Combine soups and wine; pour over chicken.
- Bake covered at 160°C for 35 minutes.
- Uncover and bake another 25 minutes.

Peachy Chicken

$^1/_2$ cup Italian dressing

2 teaspoons ground ginger

4 boneless, skinless chicken breasts

$^1/_3$ cup peach jam

- In a large plastic bag combine Italian dressing and ginger.
- Place chicken in bag and turn several times to coat chicken. Marinate in refrigerator (turning occasionally) 4 hours or overnight.
- When ready to bake remove chicken reserving $^1/_3$ cup of the marinade.
- In a small saucepan bring reserved marinade to the boil and boil for 1 minute. Remove from heat and stir in peach jam; set aside.
- In griller, grill chicken until chicken is no longer pink, brushing with marinade jam mixture the last 5 minutes of cooking.

Baked Chicken

6 boneless, skinless chicken breasts

120 g margarine, melted

$1^1/_2$ cups chicken and herb stuffing mix

- Dip chicken breast in melted margarine.
- Roll in stuffing mix to coat.
- Bake uncovered at 180°C for 45 minutes.

Glazed Chicken and Rice

4 boneless, skinless chicken breasts, cubed

1 (440 g) can pineapple pieces, undrained

1/2 cup mustard honey and herb marinade sauce

1 red capsicum, chopped

- In a frying pan with a little oil, brown chicken and cook on low heat for 15 minutes. Add the pineapple, mustard honey sauce and capsicum.
- Bring to the boil, then reduce heat to low and simmer for 10 to 15 minutes or until sauce is slightly thicened.
- Serve over hot cooked rice.

Rosemary Chicken

1 tablespoon dried rosemary, divided

1/2 cup flour

Italian dressing

3–5 boneless, skinless chicken breasts

- Combine the flour and half the rosemary together.
- Place a little Italian dressing in a shallow bowl and dip chicken breasts in dressing.
- Dredge chicken in the flour mixture. Place in a 22 × 33 cm shallow baking dish.
- Bake uncovered at 180°C for 40 minutes. Remove from oven and sprinkle remaining rosemary over breasts and cook another 10 minutes.

Chicken Dipping

$1^1/_2$ cups cornmeal flour

4 tablespoons oil

4 boneless, skinless chicken breasts

Dipping Sauce

- Mix cornmeal flour with salt and pepper to taste and 1 teaspoon dried mixed herbs.
- Add oil to the centre of a 23 × 33 cm baking pan and spread it around the entire pan.
- Cut chicken breasts into three or four pieces; dip in cornmeal mix and place in the baking pan. Arrange chicken making sure the pieces are not touching.
- Bake at 180°C uncovered for 25 minutes. Remove from oven and turn pieces over and bake another 15 minutes or until brown.

Dipping Sauce for Chicken

4 tablespoons honey

3 tablespoons spicy brown mustard

- To serve, dip chicken in dipping dsauce and enjoy.

Lemonade Chicken

6 boneless, skinless chicken breast halves

$^2/_3$ cup lemonade

$^1/_3$ cup soy sauce

1 teaspoon garlic powder

- Place chicken in a greased 23 × 33 cm baking dish.
- Combine the lemonade, soy sauce and garlic powder and pour over the chicken.
- Cover with foil and bake at 180°C for 45 minutes.
- Uncover. Spoon pan juices over chicken and cook another 10 minutes uncovered.

Classy Chicken

4 boneless, skinless chicken breasts

$^1/_4$ cup lime juice

2 teaspoons lemon pepper

60 g butter, melted

- Season chicken with salt and pepper; place in a shallow baking dish.
- Mix lime juice, lemon pepper and melted butter and pour over chicken.
- Cover and bake at 160°C for 1 hour. Remove cover for the last 15 minutes of cooking time.

Wild Rice and Chicken

1 (180 g) packet long grain and wild rice mix

4 boneless, skinless chicken breasts

4 tablespoons margarine, divided

1 large red capsicum, chopped

- Prepare rice according to packet directions.
- In a large frying pan cook chicken in 2 tablespoons of the margarine making sure each chicken breast is browned on both sides. Remove chicken and keep warm.
- Add remaining margarine to pan drippings; saute capsicum until tender. Add to the rice. Serve with the cooked chicken breast.

Mozzarella Cutlets

4 boneless, skinless chicken breast halves

1 cup herb seasoned dry breadcrumbs

1 cup prepared spaghetti sauce

4 slices mozzarella cheese

- Pound each chicken breast to flatten slightly.
- Coat well in breadcrumbs. Arrange chicken breasts in a greased 23 × 33 cm baking dish.
- Place $^1/_4$ of the sauce over each portion. Place slice of cheese over each and garnish with remaining breadcrumbs.
- Bake uncovered at 180°C for 45 minutes.

Crispy Nutty Chicken

1/3 cup dry roasted peanuts, chopped

1 cup corn flake crumbs

1/2 cup coleslaw salad dressing

5–6 chicken breasts

- Combine peanuts and corn flake crumbs on piece of wax paper.
- Pour salad dressing into a pie plate.
- Dip each piece of chicken in the salad dressing and roll in crumb mixture to coat.
- Arrange chicken in a 23 × 33 cm shallow baking dish.
- Bake uncovered at 180°C for 50 minutes until lightly brown.

Sunday Chicken

5–6 boneless, skinless chicken breast halves

1/2 cup sour cream

1/4 cup soy sauce

1 (300 mL) can French onion soup

- Place chicken in a greased 23 × 33 cm baking dish.
- In saucepan, combine the sour cream, soy sauce and soup; heat just enough to mix well. Pour over chicken breasts.
- Bake covered at 180°C for 55 minutes.

Chicken and Beef

2 (50 g) packets sliced dried beef (biltong), separated

6 strips bacon

6 boneless, skinless chicken breasts

1 (300 g) can cream of chicken soup

- Place dried beef in greased 23 × 33 cm baking dish.
- Wrap bacon strip around each chicken breast and place over beef.
- In a saucepan heat chicken soup and 1/4 cup water just until it can be poured over chicken.
- Bake covered at 160°C for 1 hour and 10 minutes.

Seasoned Chicken

4–5 boneless, skinless chicken breasts

1 tablespoon oregano

$^{3}/_{4}$ teaspoon garlic powder

$^{1}/_{3}$ cup vegetable oil

- Place chicken breasts in a plastic bag and add the oregano, garlic and oil.
- Marinate in refrigerator for 3 to 4 hours.
- Place chicken and marinade in a shallow baking dish.
- Bake covered at 160°C for 1 hour.

Ritzy Chicken

6 boneless, skinless chicken breasts

$^{1}/_{2}$ cup sour cream

1 cup cracker crumbs

$^{1}/_{4}$ teaspoon pepper

- Dip chicken in sour cream and roll in cracker crumbs with pepper mixed in.
- Place chicken in a greased shallow baking dish.
- Bake uncovered at 160°C for 55 minutes.

Chicken and Noodles

1 packet chicken flavoured instant noodles

1 (500 g) packet frozen broccoli, cauliflower and carrots

$^{2}/_{3}$ cup sweet and sour sauce

3 boneless, skinless chicken breasts, cooked, cut into thin strips

- Reserve seasoning packet from noodles. In a saucepan cook noodles and vegetables in 2 cups of boiling water for 3 minutes, stirring occasionally; drain.
- Combine noodle-vegetable mixture with seasoning packet, sweet and sour sauce and a little salt and pepper. (You may want to also add 1 tablespoon of soy sauce.)
- Add chicken and heat thoroughly.

Jiffy Chicken

8 boneless, skinless chicken breasts

$^3/_4$ cup mayonnaise

2 cups finely crushed corn flakes

$^1/_2$ cup grated parmesan cheese

- Sprinkle chicken breasts with salt and pepper.
- Dip chicken in mayonnaise and spread mayonnaise over chicken with a brush.
- Combine corn flakes and parmesan cheese. Dip mayonnaise-covered chicken in the corn flake mixture (get plenty of the crumbs on chicken) and place on a non-stick vegetable oil sprayed 23 × 33 cm heatproof ceramic dish.
- Bake uncovered at 160°C for 1 hour.

Fried Chicken and Stuffing

1 (200 g) box stuffing mix for chicken

1 (500 g) packet frozen whole corn kernels

60 g margarine

4 boneless, skinless chicken breast halves, cooked

- In a large frying pan combine contents of the seasoning packet in the stuffing mix, corn, $1^2/_3$ cups water and the margarine. Bring to the boil. Reduce heat, cover and simmer for 5 minutes.
- Stir in stuffing mix just until moistened.
- Cut chicken into thin slices. Mix with the stuffing-corn mixture.
- Cook on low heat just until thoroughly heated.

Chicken Parmesan

$1\frac{1}{2}$ cups scone mix

$\frac{1}{2}$ cup grated parmesan cheese

6–8 boneless, skinless chicken breast halves

120 g margarine, melted

- In a shallow bowl, combine scone mix and parmesan cheese.
- Dip chicken in margarine and then in scone-cheese mixture.
- Place in a large buttered baking dish. Bake uncovered at 160°C for 1 hour or until lightly browned.

Chicken Curry

2 (300 g) cans cream of mushroom soup

2 teaspoons curry powder

$\frac{1}{3}$ cup chopped almonds, toasted

4 skinless chicken breast halves, cooked, cubed

- In a large saucepan combine the soup, 1 can water, curry powder, almonds and cubed chicken.
- Heat, while stirring frequently.
- When ready to serve, spoon over cooked white rice.

Chicken Bake

8 boneless, skinless chicken breast halves

8 slices Swiss cheese

$\frac{3}{4}$ (300 g) can cream of chicken soup

1 (200 g) box chicken stuffing mix

- Flatten each chicken breast with rolling pin and place in a greased 23 × 33 cm baking dish.
- Place cheese slice over chicken. Combine chicken soup and $\frac{1}{2}$ cup water and pour over chicken.
- Mix stuffing mix as directed on box and sprinkle over chicken. Bake uncovered at 160°C for 1 hour.

Oven-Glazed Chicken

4 boneless, skinless chicken breasts

1 (300 mL) can tomato soup

2 tablespoons white wine worcestershire

2 tablespoons packed brown sugar

- Place chicken breasts in a greased 18 × 28 cm baking dish.
- In a small bowl, combine tomato soup, worcestershire and brown sugar, and mix well. Spoon over chicken.
- Bake at 180°C for 1 hour.

Chicken Supper

5 boneless, skinless chicken breasts

5 slices onion

5 potatoes, peeled and quartered

$^3/_4$ (410 g) can cream of celery soup

- Place chicken breasts in a 23 × 33 cm greased baking dish.
- Top chicken with onion slices, placing potatoes around chicken.
- Heat soup with $^1/_4$ cup water just enough to be able to pour the soup over chicken and vegetables.
- Bake covered at 160°C for 1 hour and 10 minutes.

Chicken Quesadillas

3 boneless, skinless chicken breasts, cubed

1 (40 g) packet cheese sauce, prepared to packet directions

$^2/_3$ cup chunky salsa

10 flour tortillas

- Cook chicken in frying pan until juices evaporate, stirring often.
- Add cheese sauce and salsa and heat thoroughly.
- Spread about $^1/_3$ cup chicken mixture on one-half of each tortilla to within 1 cm of edge. Moisten edge with water, fold over and seal. Place on 2 baking sheets.
- Bake at 200°C for 5 to 6 minutes.

Apricot-Ginger Chicken

2 teaspoons ground ginger

$^{1}/_{2}$ cup Italian dressing

4 boneless, skinless chicken breasts

$^{2}/_{3}$ cup apricot jam

- Combine ginger and Italian dressing; place in a large plastic bag or container. Add chicken and marinate in refrigerator overnight, turning occasionally.
- When ready to cook, remove chicken, reserving $^{1}/_{4}$ cup of the marinade. Place chicken in a shallow baking dish.
- Pour the $^{1}/_{4}$ cup of marinade in saucepan, bring to the boil and cook 1 minute. Remove from heat and stir in the jam. Set aside.
- Bake chicken on 180°C for 45 minutes; brush with marinade mixture the last 10 minutes of cooking.

Chicken Oriental

1 (200 g) jar sweet and sour sauce

1 (35 g) envelope dry onion soup mix

1 (450 g) can whole cranberry sauce

6–8 boneless, skinless chicken breasts

- In a bowl combine the sweet and sour sauce, onion soup mix and cranberry sauce.
- Place chicken breasts in an oil sprayed 23 × 33 cm shallow baking dish.
- Pour cranberry mixture over chicken breasts.
- Bake covered at 160°C for 30 minutes. Uncover and bake 25 minutes longer.

Reuben Chicken

4 boneless, skinless chicken breasts

4 slices Swiss cheese

1 (425 g) can sauerkraut, drained

1 (250 g) bottle Thousand Island salad dressing

- Arrange chicken breasts in a greased shallow baking pan.
- Place cheese over chicken and then the sauerkraut. Cover with salad dressing.
- Bake covered at 180°C for 30 minutes. Uncover and cook another 15 minutes.

Best Ever Meatloaf

500 g minced turkey

1 (200 g) packet herbed stuffing mix

2 eggs, beaten

$^1/_2$ cup ketchup, divided

- Combine the ground turkey, stuffing mix, eggs and $^1/_4$ cup of the ketchup. Mix well.
- Shape meat into an oval loaf into the centre of a 23 × 33 cm baking dish.
- Spread remaining $^1/_4$ cup of ketchup on top of loaf.
- Bake at 180°C for 1 hour.

Honey Mustard Chicken

$^1/_3$ cup Dijon mustard

$^1/_2$ cup honey

$1^1/_2$ tablespoons dried dill

1 (1.4 kg) chicken, quartered

- Combine mustard, honey and dill.
- Arrange chicken quarters in a 23 × 33 cm baking dish.
- Pour mustard mixture over chicken. Turn chicken over and make sure the mustard mixture covers the chicken.
- Bake covered at 180°C for 35 minutes. Uncover and bake aother 10 minutes.

Fried Chicken Breasts

4 boneless, skinned chicken breasts

20 saltine crackers, crushed

2 eggs, beaten

$^1/_4$ teaspoon black pepper

- Pound chicken breasts to 3 mm thickness.
- Combine eggs, pepper and 2 tablespoons water.
- Dip chicken in egg mixture and then in crushed crackers, coating well.
- Deep fry until golden brown. Drain well.

One-Dish Chicken Bake

1 (200 g) packet chicken stuffing mix

4 skinless, boneless chicken breast halves

1 (300 g) can cream of mushroom soup

$^1/_2$ cup sour cream

- Toss contents of chicken stuffing mix and $1^2/_3$ cups water into bowl and set aside. Place chicken in a greased 23 × 33 cm baking dish.
- Mix soup and sour cream in a saucepan and heat just enough to pour over chicken. Spoon stuffing evenly over top. Bake uncovered at 190°C for 40 minutes.

Sunshine Chicken

1 chicken, quartered

Flour

2 tablespoons oil

1 cup barbecue sauce mixed with $^1/_2$ cup orange juice

- Coat chicken well with flour.
- In frying pan with oil, brown chicken all over and place in a greased shallow baking pan.
- Pour barbecue sauce and orange juice over chicken.
- Bake covered at 180°C for 45 minutes. Remove from oven and spoon sauce over chicken; bake uncovered another 20 minutes.

Company Chicken

2 chickens, quartered

$1^1/_2$ (410 g) cans cream of mushroom soup

$^3/_4$ (600 mL) carton sour cream

1 cup sherry

- Place chickens in a large shallow baking dish.
- In a saucepan combine soup, sour cream and sherry. Pour mixture over chicken. (You might sprinkle a little paprika on top.)
- Bake covered at 150°C for 1 hour and 15 minutes.

Good served over rice.

Sweet 'N Spicy Chicken

500 g boneless, skinless chicken breasts, cut into 1 cm cubes

3 tablespoons taco seasoning

1 (325 g) jar chunky salsa

$^3/_4$ cup peach jam

- Place the chicken in a large resealable plastic bag; add taco seasoning and toss to coat.
- In a frying pan, brown the chicken in a little oil.
- Combine salsa and peach jam. Stir into the frying pan.
- Bring to the boil. Reduce heat and cover and simmer until the juices run clear.

Serve over rice or noodles.

Chicken Broccoli Fried

3 cups cubed, cooked chicken

1 (500 g) packet frozen broccoli florets

1 (250 g) packet processed cheddar cheese, cubed

$^2/_3$ cup mayonnaise

- In a frying pan, combine the chicken, broccoli, cheese and $^1/_4$ cup water. Cover and cook over medium heat until broccoli is crisp-tender and cheese is melted.
- Stir in mayonnaise; heat through, but do not boil.

Serve over hot cooked rice.

Tempting Chicken

3 boneless, skinless chicken breasts

3 boneless, skinless chicken thighs

1 (450 g) jar tomato-alfredo sauce

1 (300 g) can tomato soup

- In a large frying pan, brown chicken pieces in a little oil.
- Pour tomato-alfredo sauce, tomato soup and $^1/_2$ cup water over chicken pieces.
- Cover and simmer about 30 minutes.

Italian Chicken and Rice

3 boneless chicken breasts, cut into strips

1 (420 g) can chicken broth

$^3/_4$ cup uncooked rice

$^1/_4$ cup grated parmesan cheese

- Cook chicken in a non-stick frying pan until brown, stirring often. Remove chicken.
- To the frying pan add the broth and rice. Heat to boiling point. Cover and simmer over low heat for 25 minutes (check to see if it needs more water).
- Stir in cheese. Return chicken to pan. Cover and cook for 5 minutes or until done.

Sweet and Sour Chicken

1–1$^1/_2$ kg chicken pieces

Oil

1 packet dry onion soup mix

$^3/_4$ cup orange juice concentrate

- In a frying pan, brown chicken in a little oil. Place chicken in a 23 × 33 cm baking dish.
- In a small bowl, combine onion soup mix, orange juice and $^2/_3$ cup water, stirring well. Pour over chicken.
- Bake uncovered at 180°C for 50 minutes.

Chicken and Sauerkraut

6 large, boneless, skinless chicken breasts

1 (450 g) can tiny potatoes, drained

1 (450 g) can sauerkraut, drained

1/4 cup pine nuts or 1/2 teaspoon caraway seeds

- In a prepared large frying pan, season the chicken with black pepper to taste and cook over medium heat until chicken is brown on both sides, about 15 minutes.
- Add potatoes to the frying pan. Spoon sauerkraut over the potatoes. Cover and cook over low heat until chicken is done, about 35 minutes. Toast pine nuts in a dry frying pan on medium heat, stirring constantly, until golden brown. Sprinkle the chicken and sauerkraut with toasted pine nuts or caraway seeds and serve.

Option: Serve with sour cream.

Curried Chicken Casserole

1 (180 g) box chicken flavour rice-a-riso

300 g chicken tenderloins, cut into pieces

1 teaspoon curry powder

1/3 cup raisins (optional)

- In a heated frying pan add a little oil and brown the chicken pieces all over. Stir in the rice-a-riso and continue to cook as directed on the packet.
- When cooked add curry powder and raisins.
- Cover, remove from heat, stand 10 minutes before serving.

El Pronto Chicken

4 boneless, skinless chicken breasts

120 g butter, melted

$^{2}/_{3}$ cup seasoned breadcrumbs

$^{1}/_{2}$ cup grated parmesan cheese

- Dip chicken in the butter.
- Mix together the crumbs, cheese, some garlic powder, salt and pepper.
- Roll chicken in crumb-cheese mixture. Place in a greased 23 × 33 cm baking dish.
- Cover and bake at 180°C for 55 minutes.

Serve over a bed of rice.

E Z Chicken

6–8 boneless, skinless chicken breasts

1 (300 g) can cream of chicken soup

1 (85 g) packet cream cheese

1 (300 mL) carton sour cream

- Place chicken breasts in a 23 × 33 cm shallow baking dish.
- In saucepan, combine soup, cream cheese and sour cream. Heat on low just until cream cheese is melted and all three are mixed well.
- Pour mixture over chicken breasts and sprinkle chicken breasts with lemon pepper.
- Cover and bake at 150°C for 60 minutes. Uncover and bake another 15 minutes.

Serve over cooked rice.

Chicken for Lunch

4 cooked chicken breast slices from deli (thick sliced)

1 (85 g) packet cream cheese, softened

3 tablespoons salsa

2 tablespoons mayonnaise

- Place chicken slices on serving platter.
- With mixer, cream together the cream cheese, salsa and mayonnaise. Place a heaped tablespoon on top of chicken slices.

Serve cold.

Sesame Chicken

120 g margarine, melted

2 teaspoons chilli powder

4 skinless, boneless chicken breast halves

1 cup sesame seeds, lightly toasted

- Combine margarine and chilli powder. Dip chicken in margarine mixture then roll in the sesame seeds.
- Place in a buttered 23 × 33 cm baking dish. Bake uncovered at 160°C for 1 hour, turning after 30 minutes.

Turkey and Noodles

2½ cups diced cooked turkey

1 (250 g) packet noodles

1 packet chicken gravy, prepared

2 cups cracker crumbs

- Boil noodles according to directions on packet; drain.
- Arrange alternate layers of noodles, turkey and gravy in greased 2 litre baking dish. Cover with crumbs.
- Bake uncovered at 180°C for 35 minutes.

Adobe Chicken

2 cups cooked brown rice

¾ (425 g) can diced tomatoes with garlic and black pepper

3 cups chopped, cooked chicken

1½ (500 g) packets shredded cheddar cheese, divided

- Combine rice, tomatoes, chicken and half of the cheese.
- Spoon into a buttered 18 × 28 cm baking dish. Cook covered at 160°C for 30 minutes.
- Uncover, sprinkle remaining cheese over casserole and return to oven for 5 minutes.

Duck with Cherry Sauce

2–2$\frac{1}{2}$ kg duckling

1 (750 g) jar cherry jam

2 tablespoons red wine vinegar

- Prick skin of duckling. Place breast side down on a rack in a shallow roasting pan.
- Bake uncovered at 160°C for 2 hours or when a meat thermometer reads 180°. Drain fat from the pan.
- Cover and let stand for 20 minutes before carving.

For the sauce combine, cherry jam and vinegar in a small saucepan. Heat and stir over medium heat until heated through. Serve with the duck.

Smothered Steak

750 g round steak

1 (300 g) can cream of mushroom soup

1 envelope dry onion soup mix

$\frac{2}{3}$ cup milk

- Cut steak into serving-size pieces and place in a well greased 23 × 33 cm baking pan.
- In a saucepan mix soup, dry onion soup and milk. Heat just enough to be able to mix well. Pour over steak.
- Seal with foil. Bake at 160°C for 1 hour.

Steak Bake Italiano

1 kg lean round steak

2 teaspoons Italian herb seasoning

1 teaspoon garlic salt

2 (400 g) cans diced tomatoes

- Cut the steak into serving-size pieces and brown in a frying pan.
- Place in a 23 × 33 cm baking dish.
- Combine Italian seasoning, garlic salt and diced tomatoes. Pour over steak pieces.
- Cover and bake at 160°C for 1 hour.

Tomato Garlic Steak

1 (420 g) can tomato soup

$^{1}/_{2}$ cup Italian salad dressing

$^{1}/_{3}$ cup water

3–4 boneless beef sirloin steaks

- In a saucepan, combine soup, dressing and water with 2 cloves crushed garlic.
- Grill steaks to desired doneness; allow 15 minutes for medium. Turn once and brush often with the sauce.
- Heat remaining sauce to serve with steak.

Savoury Rib Roast

1 tablespoon dried thyme

1 tablespoon dried, crushed rosemary

1 teaspoon rubbed sage

1 ($2^1/_2$ kg) rib roast

- In small bowl, combine the thyme, rosemary and sage and rub over roast. Place roast, fat side up.
- On a rack in a large roasting pan. Bake uncovered at 180°C for 2–$2^1/_2$ hours or until meat reaches desired doneness.
- Remove roast to a warm serving platter and let stand 10 minutes before slicing.

Southwestern Steak

300 g tenderised round steak

1 (400 g) can diced tomatoes

$^3/_4$ cup picante sauce

2 teaspoons beef stock powder

- Cut beef into serving-size pieces and dredge in flour.
- In a frying pan, brown steak in a little oil.
- Mix tomatoes, picante sauce and beef stock and pour over steak.
- Cover and simmer on low heat for 50 minutes or until meat is tender.

Baked Onion-Mushroom Steak

750 g round steak, (1 cm thick)

Salt and pepper

1 (300 g) can cream of mushroom soup

1 envelope dry onion soup mix

- Place steak in a greased 23 × 33 cm baking dish. Sprinkle with salt and pepper.
- Pour mushroom soup and $^1/_2$ cup water over steak and sprinkle with onion soup mix.
- Cover and bake at 160°C for 2 hours.

Red Wine Round Steak

1 kg (1.5 cm thick) round steak

1 packet dry onion soup mix

1 cup dry red wine

1 (125 g) can sliced mushrooms

- Remove all fat from steak and cut in serving-size pieces. Brown meat in a frying pan with a little oil on both sides. Place steak in a buttered 23 × 33 cm casserole dish.
- In a frying pan combine the onion soup mix, wine, 1 cup hot water and mushrooms. Pour over browned steak.
- Cover and bake for 1 hour 20 minutes or until steak is tender.

Round Steak Simmer

1½ kg (1 cm thick) round steak

Flour, oil

2 (410 g) cans cream of tomato soup

2 onions, thinly sliced

- Cut steak into serving-size pieces. Dust with flour and a little salt and pepper. In a frying pan brown meat in a little oil.
- Mix onions and soup with 1 can water and add to steak. Bring to the boil.
- Turn heat down and simmer for 1 hour 20 minutes.

Casserole Supper

500 g lean minced beef

¼ cup uncooked white rice

1 (40 g) packet French onion soup

Fried onion rings

- Brown ground beef, drain and place in a buttered 18 × 28 cm baking dish.
- Mix in the rice, onion soup mix and 1 cup water. Cover and bake at 180°C for 40 minutes.
- Uncover and sprinkle onion rings over top; return to oven for 5–10 minutes more.

Beef and Broccoli

500 g beef sirloin steak

1 onion, chopped

$^{3}/_{4}$ (410 g) can cream of celery soup

1 (500 g) packet frozen, chopped broccoli, thawed

- Slice beef across the grain into very thin strips. In a large frying pan brown steak strips and onion in a little hot oil, while stirring.
- Reduce heat, stir in soup and broccoli and simmer for 10 minutes.
- When ready to serve, spoon beef mixture over hot, cooked noodles.

Beef and Noodles

$1^{1}/_{2}$ kg lean beef, cubed

2 (410 g) cans cream of mushroom soup

$^{1}/_{2}$ cup cooking sherry

1 (35 g) packet dry onion soup mix

- Mix all ingredients adding $^{1}/_{4}$ cup water. Pour into a 3 litre baking dish.
- Bake at 180°C for about 2 hours.

Serve over noodles.

Easy Roast

2 kg rump roast

1 (300 g) can cream of mushroom soup

1 (35 g) packet dry onion soup mix

$^{1}/_{2}$ cup white wine

- Place roast in a roasting pan.
- Combine mushroom soup, onion soup mix and white wine and $^{1}/_{3}$ cup water. Pour over roast.
- Cover roast with foil and bake at 160°C for about 3 to 4 hours.

Supper-Ready Beef

1 (2 kg) rump roast

1 (300 g) can French onion soup

1 (400 g) packet beef stock

1 teaspoon garlic powder

- Place roast in a roasting pan.
- Pour soup and stock over roast and sprinkle with garlic powder.
- Place lid on roasting pan and bake at 180°C for 2½ hours.
- Gravy will be in pan.

Rump Roast

1 (1½–2 kg) boneless rump roast

4 medium potatoes, peeled, cut into pieces

2 onions, quartered

1 (410 g) can mushroom soup

- Place roast in a roaster; season with seasoned salt and pepper, cover.
- Bake at 180°C for about 1 hour.
- Uncover; add potates and onions. Continue cooking for half an hour.
- Heat soup in a saucepan and pour over roast and vegetables. Return to oven and cook 20 to 30 minutes more until meat is cooked.

Easy Salisbury Steak

500 g lean minced beef

½ cup flour

1 egg

1 (375 g) carton brown onion and garlic gravy

- In a large bowl, combine beef, flour and egg. Add a little seasoned salt and pepper; mix well.
- Shape into 5 patties and place in a shallow 18 × 28 cm baking dish.
- Bake uncovered at 180°C for 20 minutes; drain off any fat.
- Pour beef gravy over patties. Bake another 20 minutes.

Serve with rice or noodles.

Onion-Beef Dinner

$1\frac{1}{2}$ kg lean minced beef

1 packet dry onion soup mix

$\frac{1}{2}$ cup water

1 (410 g) can French onion soup

- Combine beef, soup mix and water. Stir well and shape into patties about 1 cm thick.
- Heat in a large non-stick frying pan and brown patties on both sides.
- Pour the soup over the patties, reduce heat and simmer for 35 minutes.

A Wicked Meatloaf

1 (200 g) packet herbed stuffing mix

1 egg

$\frac{1}{2}$ cup salsa

750 g lean minced beef

- In a bowl combine stuffing mix, egg, salsa and $\frac{1}{3}$ cup water; mix well.
- Add minced beef to the stuffing mixture.
- Spoon into a 23 × 13 cm loaf pan.
- Bake at 180°C for 1 hour.

Smothered Beef Steak

1 kg lean round steak

1 cup uncooked rice

1 (55 g) hearty beef cup of soup, prepared to packet directions

1 green capsicum, chopped

- Cut steak into serving-size pieces and brown in a very large frying pan.
- Add the rice, beef soup, capsicum and 1 cup water to the frying pan. Bring to the boil. Reduce heat and cover; simmer for 1 hour.

Smothered Beef Patties

750 g minced beef

$^1/_2$ cup chilli sauce

$^1/_2$ cup buttery cracker crumbs

1 (375 mL) carton beef stock

- Combine beef, chilli sauce and cracker crumbs and form into 5 or 6 patties. In a frying pan, brown patties and pour beef stock over patties.
- Bring to the boil. Reduce heat and cover; simmer for about 40 minutes.

Savoury Herb Meat Loaf

650 g minced round beef, browned

1 (410 g) can each cream of mushroom soup and cream of celery soup

1 (35 g) packet dry onion soup mix

$1^1/_2$ cups cooked rice

- Mix all ingredients together.
- Place into a 23 × 33 cm baking dish and form a loaf.
- Bake at 180°C for 50 minutes.

Mexican Casserole

1 (400 g) bag tortilla chips, divided

1 kg lean minced beef

1 (400 g) can diced tomatoes

1 (250 g) packet shredded cheddar cheese mixed with 1 teaspoon Mexican style chilli powder or to taste

- Partially crush half bag of chips and place in bottom of a buttered 23 × 33 cm baking dish.
- Brown minced beef and drain.
- Add diced tomatoes, cheese and chilli powder and mix well. Sprinkle finely crushed chips over top of casserole.
- Bake uncovered at 180°C for 40 minutes.

Beef Patties in Creamy Onion Sauce

750 g lean ground beef

1/3 cup salsa

1/3 cup butter cracker crumbs

1 (300 g) can cream of onion soup or a 375 mL carton brown onion and garlic gravy

- Combine beef, salsa and cracker crumbs and form into 5–6 patties. Brown in frying pan and reduce heat.
- Add 1/4 cup water and simmer for 15 minutes. In a saucepan combine onion soup and 1/2 cup water or milk; heat and mix.
- Pour over beef patties. Serve over hot, cooked noodles.

Next-Day Beef

1 (2 1/2–3 kg) trimmed beef brisket

1 packet dry onion soup mix

1 (300 g) bottle ketchup

1 (340 g) bottle barbecue sauce

- Place brisket, cut side up, in a roasting pan.
- In a bowl, combine onion soup mix, ketchup and barbecue sauce. Pour over brisket.
- Cover and cook at 160°C for 4–5 hours or until tender. Remove brisket from pan and pour off drippings.
- Trim all the fat from meat, slice. Skim fat off the drippings and serve sauce over brisket.

Easy Breezy Brisket

1 (2–2 1/2 kg) beef brisket

1 envelope dry onion soup mix

2 tablespoons worcestershire sauce

1 cup red wine

- Place brisket in a shallow baking pan.
- Sprinkle onion soup over the brisket.
- Pour worcestershire sauce and red wine in the pan.
- Cover and bake at 160°C for 5 to 6 hours.

Slow Cookin', Good Tastin' Brisket

1 (2–2$^1/_2$ kg) beef brisket

1 (150 g) bottle worcestershire sauce

1$^1/_4$ cup barbecue sauce with hickory

- Pour $^1/_4$ cup barbecue sauce over brisket. Cover and refrigerate overnight.
- Drain. Pour worcestershire sauce over brisket.
- Cover and bake at 140°C for 6–7 hours.
- Cover with barbecue sauce. Bake uncovered for another 30 minutes. Slice very thin across the grain.

Taste of the Irish Corned Beef

1 (2–2$^1/_2$ kg) corned beef brisket

4 large potatoes, peeled, quartered

6 carrots, peeled, halved

1 head cabbage

- Place corned beef in roaster, cover with water. Bring to the boil. Turn heat down and simmer 3 hours, adding water if necessary.
- Add potatoes and carrots. Cut cabbage into eighths and lay over top of other vegetables.
- Bring to the boil; turn heat down and cook another 30 to 40 minutes, until vegetables are done. When slightly cool, slice corned beef across the grain.

Sweet Corned Beef

1 ($2^1/_2$ kg) corned beef brisket

Whole cloves

$^1/_2$ cup maple syrup

$^1/_4$ teaspoon black pepper

- Place corned beef in a large saucepan with water to cover beef. Bring to the boil. Lower the heat and simmer until done, allowing 50 minutes per 500 g.
- When corned beef has cooked, place on a rack in a shallow pan. Stick the whole cloves in a crosswise design.
- Pour syrup over meat and sprinkle with black pepper.
- Place in oven at 190°C to brown and glaze for about 15 minutes. When ready to serve, slice beef across the grain. Serve hot or at room temperature.

Serve with creamed cabbage.

Meat and Potato Stew

1 kg beef stewing meat, cubed

2 (420 g) cans new potatoes, drained

1 (420 g) can sliced carrots, drained

1 (300 g) can French onion soup

- In large pot, cook stewing meat with about 2 cups water for 1 hour.
- Add the potatoes, carrots and onion soup and mix. Heat to boiling, reduce heat and simmer for 30 minutes.

Chihuahua Dogs

1 (300 g) bottle chilli sauce

1 (10 count) packet frankfurts

10 preformed taco shells

Shredded cheddar cheese

- Pour chilli sauce into a saucepan and heat.
- Place a frankfurt in each taco shell. Top with the heated chilli sauce and cheese; onions and tomatoes if you like.
- Place in microwave and heat for 30 seconds or until the frankfurts are warm.

Slow Cook Stew

1 kg stewing meat, cubed

1 envelope dry onion soup mix

1 (410 g) can mushroom soup

1 (300 mL) carton sour cream

- Brown meat cubes in a roasting pan.
- Combine soup mix, mushroom soup and $1^1/_2$ cans water. Pour over stewing meat. Cover tightly.
- Bake at 140°C for 6–8 hours. When ready to serve, stir in sour cream. Return mixture to oven until heated thoroughly. Serve over noodles.

This will be great in a slow cooker while you are at work or overnight while you sleep.

Texas Chilli Pie

3 (400 g) cans savoury mince

1 (500 g) packet small corn chips

1 onion, chopped

1 (500 g) packet shredded cheddar cheese

- Heat savoury mince in saucepan.
- In a 23 × 33 cm baking dish, layer the corn chips, mince, onion and cheese $^1/_3$ at a time. Repeat layers with cheese on top.
- Bake at 160°C for 20 minutes or until cheese bubbles.

'Giddy-Up' Pork Chops

6 boneless pork chops

$^1/_2$ cup salsa

$^1/_2$ cup honey or packed brown sugar

1 teaspoon soy sauce

- Brown pork chops in an oven-proof pan.
- Combine salsa, honey or brown sugar and soy sauce and heat for 20–30 seconds in microwave oven. Pour salsa mixture over pork chops, cover and bake at 160°C for about 45 minutes or until pork chops are tender.

Variation: $^1/_4$ teaspoon crushed red pepper flakes.

Pork Chops in Cream Gravy

4 ($^1/_2$ cm thick) pork chops

Flour

Oil

$2^1/_4$ cups whole milk

- Dip chops in flour with a little salt and pepper. Brown pork chops on both sides in a little oil. Remove chops from pan.
- Add about 2 tablespoons flour to frying pan and brown lightly; stir in a little salt and pepper. Slowly stir in milk to make gravy. Return chops to frying pan with the gravy.
- Cover and simmer on low burner for about 40 minutes.

Serve over rice or noodles.

Pork-Potato Chop

6 boneless or loin pork chops, seasoned with salt and pepper

1 (375 mL) carton chicken stock

2 (35 g) packets dry onion gravy mix

4 red potatoes, sliced

- Brown pork chops in a large frying pan.
- Combine chicken broth and gravy mix. Place potatoes with pork chops and pour the gravy mixture over the pork chops and potatoes.
- Heat to boiling, cover and simmer about 45 minutes or until the pork chops and potatoes are fork-tender.

Cranberries and Pork Chops

6–8 thick pork chops

Flour

2 cups frozen cranberries

1 cup sugar

- Coat the pork chops in flour; brown in a small amount of oil in a frying pan. Place in a shallow baking dish.
- Add the cranberries, sugar and $^1/_2$ cup water.
- Cover. Bake at 180°C for 30 minutes. Uncover and continue baking for another 30 minutes.

Mexicali Pork Chops

1 envelope taco seasoning

4 (1 cm thick) boneless pork loin chops

1 tablespoon oil

Salsa

- Rub taco seasoning over pork chops.
- In a frying pan, brown pork chops in oil over medium heat.
- Add 2 tablespoons water; turn heat to low and simmer pork chops about 40 minutes. Check to see if a little more water is needed.
- Spoon salsa over pork chops to serve.

Chops and Stuffing

1 (200 g) box savoury herb stuffing mix

6 centre-cut pork chops

Oil

3 onions, halved

- Make stuffing according to packet directions and set aside.
- Fry pork chops in a pan with a little oil. Brown chops on both sides and place in a greased 23 × 33 cm baking dish.
- Divide stuffing and onions among pork chops and mound on top of each.
- Cover and bake at 180°C for about 30 minutes.

Apple Pork Chops

4 butterflied pork chops

2 apples, peeled, halved and cored

2 teaspoons margarine

2 tablespoons brown sugar

- Place pork chops in a non-stick, oil sprayed shallow baking dish. Season with salt and pepper.
- Cover and bake at 180°C for 30 minutes. Uncover, and place apple halves on top of pork chops. Add a little margarine and a little brown sugar on each of these apples.
- Bake for another 15 minutes.

Pork Chops, Potatoes and Green Beans

6–8 boneless or loin pork chops

2 (30 g) packets gravy mix or 2 (375 g) cartons prepared gravy

2 (440 g) cans white potatoes, drained

2 (440 g) cans cut green beans, drained

- Season pork chops with salt and pepper if desired. Brown pork chops in large, non-stick Dutch oven.
- Mix the gravy with water as directed or pour the prepared gravy over the pork chops. Cover and simmer for 30 minutes.
- Add the potatoes and green beans and simmer about 10 minutes or until the pork chops are tender and the green beans and potatoes are heated through.

Baked Pork Chops

$^3/_4$ cup ketchup

$^3/_4$ cup packed brown sugar

$^1/_4$ cup lemon juice

4 butterflied pork chops

- Combine ketchup, $^1/_2$ cup water, brown sugar and lemon juice.
- Place pork chops in a 18 × 28 cm buttered baking dish and pour sauce over pork chops.
- Bake covered at 160°C for 50 minutes.

Spicy Pork Chops

4–6 pork chops

1 large onion

1 capsicum

1 (400 g) can diced tomatoes with onion, garlic and basil

- Brown pork chops in a frying pan with a little oil.
- Spray casserole dish with non-stick spray. Place chops in dish.
- Cut onion and capsicum into large chunks and place on chops. Pour tomato and green chillies over chops; sprinkle 1 teaspoon salt over casserole.
- Bake covered at 180°C for 45 minutes.

Pork Chop Dinner

4 medium potatoes, peeled

2 large onions, sliced

4–6 medium thick pork chops

Milk

- Peel and thinly slice potatoes and onions.
- Place a layer of potatoes in the bottom of a 23 × 33 cm baking dish, sprinkle with salt and pepper. Place a layer of onions in dish and sprinkle with salt and pepper.
- Arrange pork chops on top, sprinkle with salt and pepper.
- Carefully pour the milk into dish until it is about 1 cm deep. Cover dish with foil sealing around edges.
- Bake covered at 160°C for 1 hour. Uncover and bake 15 minutes more to brown chops.

Sweet and Sour Spareribs

2 kg pork spareribs

$^{1}/_{3}$ cup lemon cordial

$^{1}/_{2}$ teaspoon garlic salt

$^{1}/_{3}$ cup soy sauce

- Place ribs, meaty side down in a shallow roasting pan. Cook covered at 180°C for 40 minutes.
- Remove cover, drain fat and return ribs to oven. Bake 30 minutes more. Drain fat again.
- Combine remaining ingredients and brush on ribs.
- Reduce temperature to 160°C. Cover and bake for 1 more hour or until tender, brushing occasionally with sauce.

Saucy Pork Chops

4 (1 cm thick) pork chops

1 tablespoon oil

1 (400 g) can cream of mushroom soup

2 tablespoons soy sauce

- In frying pan, brown pork chops in oil and cook about 15 minutes; drain.
- Add soup and soy sauce. Heat to the boil.
- Return chops to pan. Reduce heat to low. Cover and simmer about 20 minutes.

Honey Ham Slice

$^{1}/_{3}$ cup orange juice

$^{1}/_{3}$ cup honey

1 teaspoon prepared mustard

1 ($2^{1}/_{2}$ cm thick) slice fully cooked ham, centre cut

- Combine orange juice, honey and mustard in a saucepan and cook slowly for 10 minutes, stirring occasionally.
- Place ham in a grilling pan about 7 cm from heat. Brush with orange glaze.
- Grill 8 minutes on first side. Turn ham slice over. Brush with glaze again and grill another 6 to 8 minutes.

Cran-Apple Ham

1 cup apple juice, divided

1 tablespoon cornstarch

1 cup whole cranberry sauce

1 centre-cut ham slice or 1 (1–1½ kg) smoked, boneless ham

- In a medium saucepan over low heat, pour in ¼ cup apple juice and cornstarch and stir until the cornstarch is smooth. Add the remaining apple juice. Using medium heat, bring to the boil and cook, stirring constantly, until the mixture clears and has thickened.
- Stir in the cranberry sauce and heat 2–3 minutes.
- Place the ham slice in a shallow baking pan. Spread sauce over the ham slice and bake at 180°C about 20–30 minutes, basting the ham with the sauce 2–3 times.
- Serve warmed sauce with the ham. (If you use the boneless ham in the recipe, cook 45–60 minutes longer.)

Optional: Add ½ teaspoon lemon juice, pinch of ground cinnamon or dash of ground cloves.

Orange Pork Chops

6–8 medium thick pork chops

60 g margarine

2¼ cups orange juice

2 tablespoons orange marmalade

- Brown both sides of pork chops in margarine in hot frying pan adding salt and pepper.
- Pour orange juice over chops. Cover and simmer until done about 1 hour but time will vary with the thickness of the pork chops. Add more orange juice if necessary.
- During the last few minutes of cooking add 2 tablespoons of orange marmalade.

This makes a delicious gravy to serve over rice.

Pork Chops and Fried Rice

4–6 boneless pork chops

1 (300 g) packet frozen fried rice, thawed

$^{1}/_{3}$ cup frozen peas

3 green onions (shallots) with tops, sliced

- Dry pork chops and brown over medium heat in a preheated, prepared large frying pan. Add $^{1}/_{4}$ cup water and simmer until tender, adding water if needed.
- Remove the pork chops from the pan and keep warm.
- In a medium bowl, mix the fried rice and $^{1}/_{4}$ cup water. Add the fried rice to the pan and heat for 10 minutes.
- Add the peas and green onions to rice and cook an additional 5 minutes or until peas are crisp-tender.
- Serve the pork chops with the fried rice.

Hawaiian Pork

1 kg lean pork tenderloin, cut in $2^{1}/_{2}$ cm cubes

1 (440 g) can pineapple pieces, undrained

1 (340 g) bottle chilli sauce

1 teaspoon ground ginger

- In a frying pan, season pork cubes with salt and pepper.
- Combine meat, pineapple with juice, chilli sauce and ginger.
- Simmer covered for $1^{1}/_{2}$ hours.

Serve over rice.

Ham and Sweet Potatoes

3 tablespoons Dijon-style mustard, divided

1 ($1\frac{1}{2}$–2 kg) boneless smoked ham

$\frac{1}{2}$ cup honey or packed brown sugar

4 cooked sweet potatoes, quartered

- Preheat oven at 160°C. Spread 2 tablespoons mustard on the ham. Place ham in prepared shallow baking pan and bake for 20 minutes.
- Combine the remaining mustard with the brown sugar or honey and spread over the ham.
- Add the sweet potatoes, baste with the sauce and bake for 20 minutes.

Mustard Ham

1 ($2\frac{1}{2}$ cm) thick centre-cut slice smoked leg ham (about $1\frac{1}{2}$ kg)

2 teaspoons dry mustard

$\frac{1}{3}$ cup honey

$\frac{1}{3}$ cup cooking wine

- Rub ham slice with the dry mustard, using 1 teaspoon mustard for each side. Place in a shallow baking pan.
- Combine honey and wine; pour over ham.
- Bake uncovered at 180°C for about 35 minutes.

Supper in a Dish

1 (180 g) packet Rice-a-Riso

$1\frac{1}{2}$ cups cubed, cooked ham

$1\frac{1}{2}$ cups shredded cheddar cheese

1 (250 g) can green peas

- Prepare rice according to directions on packet.
- In a large bowl, combine rice, ham, cheese and peas.
- Pour into a 3 litre baking dish and bake at 180°C for 15 to 20 minutes.

Ham and Veggies

2 (500 g) packets frozen mixed vegetables

1 (410 g) can cream of celery soup

3 cups cubed, cooked ham

½ teaspoon dried basil

- Cook vegetables as directed on packet.
- Add soup, ham and basil.
- Cook until thoroughly heated. Serve hot.

Peach-Pineapple Baked Ham

1½–2 kg boneless smoked ham

4 tablespoons Dijon-style mustard, divided

1 cup peach jam

1 cup pineapple jam

- Preheat oven to 160°C. Spread 2 tablespoons mustard on the ham.
- Place ham in a prepared, shallow baking pan and bake for 20 minutes.
- Combine the remaining 2 tablespoons mustard and both jams and heat in the microwave oven for 20 seconds (or in a small saucepan at low heat for 2–3 minutes).
- Pour over the ham and bake for about 15 minutes.

Ham Patties

2 cups minced ham

2 eggs, slightly beaten

1 cup cracker crumbs

- Combine ham, eggs, cracker crumbs and a little pepper. Shape into patties.
- Place a little oil in a heavy frying pan and sauté patties until golden brown.

This is a great way to use leftover ham.

Spunky Spareribs

$2\frac{1}{2}$–3 kg pork spareribs
$\frac{2}{3}$ cup orange juice concentrate, undiluted
2 teaspoons worcestershire sauce
$\frac{1}{2}$ teaspoon garlic powder

- Place spareribs in a shallow baking pan, meaty side down. Sprinkle with a little salt and pepper.
- Roast at 190°C for 30 minutes.
- Turn ribs and roast another 30 minutes. Drain off fat.
- Combine remaining ingredients and brush the mixture on ribs.
- Reduce heat to 150°C. Cover ribs and roast 2 hours or until tender, basting occasionally.

Orange Spareribs

2–$2\frac{1}{2}$ kg pork spareribs
$\frac{2}{3}$ cup orange juice concentrate
$\frac{1}{2}$ teaspoon garlic salt
$\frac{2}{3}$ cup honey

- Place ribs, meaty side down in a shallow roasting pan. Bake at 180°C for 30 minutes. Drain off fat and turn ribs. Bake 30 minutes more.
- Combine remaining ingredients and brush on ribs. Reduce temperature to 160°C. Cover pan and bake $1\frac{1}{2}$ hours or until tender, brushing with sauce several times.

Barbecued Spareribs

$1^1/_2$–2 kg pork spareribs or American-style pork ribs, trimmed

1 cup hot ketchup or chilli sauce

$^1/_2$ cup honey or packed brown sugar

- Place spareribs on a rack in a baking pan and bake at 180°C for $1^1/_2$ hours.
- Combine ketchup, honey or brown sugar in a small saucepan and simmer for 2–3 minutes.
- Baste the spareribs on both sides generously with the ketchup mixture.
- Bake spareribs an additional $1^1/_2$ hours or until tender, basting generously every 15–20 minutes.

German-Style Ribs and Kraut

$1^1/_2$–2 kg pork ribs or American-style pork ribs

3 potatoes, peeled, cubed or sliced

2 (500 g) cans sauerkraut, drained

$^1/_4$ cup pine nuts, toasted

- In a prepared Dutch oven or heavy based saucepan, brown ribs on all sides. Pepper ribs to taste and add 1 cup water.
- Bring to the boil, turn down heat and simmer about 2 hours until ribs are very tender.
- Add potaotes and cook on low heat for 20 minutes. Add sauerkraut and continue cooking until potatoes are done.
- Sprinkle pine nuts or caraway seeds on the ribs and sauerkraut immediately before serving.

Tequila Baby Back Ribs

2 kg American-style pork spareribs

1 (340 g) bottle tequila lime marinade, or other of choice, divided

Black pepper

- Cut ribs in lengths and place in a non-metallic container.
- Add 3/4 cup marinade; turn to coat. Marinate in refrigerator overnight. Place ribs in a shallow baking dish coated with vegetable oil spray; discard used marinade.
- Cover ribs with foil and bake at 190°C for 30 minutes.
- Remove from oven and spread a little of the extra marinade over ribs. Lower heat to 150°C and cook for 1 hour.
- Uncover to let ribs brown; bake 30 minutes longer.

Plum Peachy Pork Roast

1 (2–2 1/2 kg) boneless pork loin roast

1/2 cup plum jam

1/2 cup peach jam

1/2 teaspoon ginger

- Place roast in a shallow baking pan and bake at 160°C for about 35 minutes. Turn roast to brown the other side and bake another 35 minutes.
- In a saucepan heat the plum and peach jams and ginger.
- When roast is finished cooking brush roast generously with jam mixture.
- Bake and baste another 15 minutes.

Pork Tenderloin

1½ kg pork tenderloin

1 (400 g) can diced tomatoes

1 packet vegetable and herb soup mix

2 tablespoons worcestershire sauce

- Place tenderloin strips in roasting dish.
- Mix remaining ingredients; spread over meat.
- Bake covered at 160°C for 1 hour and 20 minutes.

Tenderloin with Apricot Sauce

1½ kg pork tenderloin

1 cup apricot jam

⅓ cup lemon juice, ⅓ cup ketchup

1 tablespoon soy sauce

- Place tenderloins in roasting dish.
- Combine jam, lemon juice, ketchup and soy sauce.
- Pour over pork and bake covered at 160°C for 1 hour and 20 minutes. Baste once during cooking.

Serve over white rice.

Pork Picante

500 g pork tenderloin, cubed

2 tablespoons taco seasoning

1 cup chunky salsa

⅓ cup peach jam

- Toss pork with the taco seasoning and brown with a little oil in a frying pan.
- Stir in salsa and jam. Bring to the boil.
- Lower heat and simmer for 30 minutes.

Pour over hot cooked rice.

Apple-Topped Tenderloin

$1^1/_2$ cups hickory marinade, divided

1 ($1^1/_2$–2 kg) pork tenderloin

1 (450 g) can pie apple

$^3/_4$ teaspoon cinnamon

- In a plastic bag combine 1 cup marinade and tenderloin; seal bag. Marinade in refrigerator for at least 1 hour.
- Remove tenderloin; discard used marinade.
- Cook tenderloin uncovered at 160°C for 1 hour, basting twice with $^1/_4$ cup of the remaining marinade. Let stand 10 or 15 minutes before slicing. In a saucepan combine pie filling, the extra $^1/_4$ cup marinade and cinnamon; heat.

Serve heated apples over sliced tenderloin.

Italian Sausage and Ravioli

500 g sweet Italian pork sausage, casing removed

1 (500 g) jar extra chunky mushroom spaghetti sauce

1 (750 g) chilled or frozen spinach and cheese filled ravioli, cooked and drained

Grated parmesan cheese

- In a roasting pan, over medium heat, cook sausage in a hot frying pan until browned and no longer pink, stirring to separate meat.
- Stir in spaghetti sauce. Heat to boiling.
- Add ravioli. Heat through, stirring occasionally.
- Pour into serving dish and sprinkle with parmesan cheese.

Sausage Casserole

500 g pork sausage

2 (425 g) cans pork and baked beans

1 (425 g) can diced tomatoes with onions and garlic

1 packet scone mix

- Brown sausage and drain fat.
- Add beans and tomatoes and mix. Bring to the boil. Pour into a 3 litre greased casserole dish.
- Prepare scone mix according to packet. Drop by spoonfuls over meat and bean mixture.
- Bake at 200°C for 30 minutes or until top is browned.

Tangy Pork Chops

4–6 pork chops

1/4 cup worcestershire sauce

1/4 cup ketchup

1/2 cup honey

- In frying pan, brown pork chops. Place in a shallow baking dish.
- Combine worcestershire, ketchup and honey. Pour over pork chops.
- Cover and bake at 160°C for 45 minutes.

Sweet and Savoury Pork Chops

6–8 (1 1/2–2 cm thick) boneless pork chops, trimmed

1/2 cup grape, apple or plum jam

1/2 cup chilli sauce or hot ketchup

Soy sauce

- Brown pork chops and season to taste with salt and pepper. Transfer browned pork chops to a shallow baking dish, place in oven and bake at 160°C for 30 minutes.
- Combine jam and chilli sauce or ketchup and spread over the pork chops. Cook for 15 minutes, baste with the sauce and cook 15 minutes more or until pork chops are tender. Serve with soy sauce.

Grilled Lemon-Garlic Prawns

500 g raw prawns, peeled and deveined

1 teaspoon garlic salt

2 tablespoons lemon juice

2 tablespoons butter

- Place prawns in a shallow baking pan.
- Sprinkle with garlic salt and lemon juice; dot with butter.
- Grill on one side for 3 minutes. Turn and grill 3 minutes more.

If the prawns are large, split them down the middle and spread them out like a butterfly, then season.

Fried Prawns

2 teaspoons olive oil

1 kg raw prawns, peeled and deveined

2/3 cup herb and garlic marinade with lemon juice

1/4 cup finely chopped green onions (shallots) with tops

- In large non-stick frying pan, heat oil. Add prawns and marinade.
- Cook, stirring often until prawns turn pink. Stir in green onions.

Serve over hot, cooked rice or your favourite pasta.

Beer-Batter Prawns

1 (340 mL) can beer

1 cup flour

2 teaspoons garlic powder

500 g green prawns, peeled, veined

- Make batter by mixing beer, flour and garlic powder and stir to a creamy consistency.
- Dip prawns into batter to cover and deep fry in hot oil.

Boiled Prawns

1½ kg fresh green prawns

1 teaspoon salt

2 teaspoons seafood seasoning

½ cup vinegar

- Half fill a large saucepan with water, add salt, seasoning and vinegar and bring to a rapid boil.
- Add the green prawns, a few at a time. Bring back to the boil and cook for 1 to 2 minutes until the shells turn completely pink and prawns begin to rise to the surface.
- Drain quickly and plunge into cold water. Drain and refrigerate.

Crab Mornay

2 (170 g) cans crabmeat, drained, flaked

1 cup cream of mushroom soup

½ cup shredded Swiss cheese

½ cup seasoned breadcrumbs

- Preheat oven to 180°C.
- Combine crabmeat, soup and cheese.
- Pour into a prepared 1½ litre casserole dish and sprinkle with breadcrumbs.
- Bake uncovered for 30 minutes or until soup is bubbling and breadcrumbs are lightly browned.

Prawn Supper

750 g cooked and peeled prawns

1 small head lettuce, chopped

1 (400 g) can artichokes, quartered, drained

1 avocado, sliced

- Combine all ingredients and serve with a creamy salad dressing.

Seafood Delight

1 (200 g) can prawns, drained

1 (170 g) can crabmeat, drained, flaked

1 (300 g) can creamed corn

2–3 cups seasoned fresh breadcrumbs, divided

- Preheat the oven to 180°C. Mix the prawns, crabmeat, corn and $^1/_3$ cup breadcrumbs.
- Place in a prepared $1^1/_2$ litre casserole dish. Sprinkle with the remaining breadcrumbs.
- Bake for 30 minutes or until the casserole is bubbling and the breadcrumbs are lightly browned.

Curried Red Snapper

750 g fresh red snapper

2 medium onions, 2 celery ribs, chopped

1 teaspoon curry powder

$^1/_4$ cup milk

- Place snapper in a greased 23 × 33 cm baking pan.
- In frying pan, sauté onions and celery in a little margarine. Add curry powder and a little salt, mixing well. Remove from heat; stir in milk. Spoon over snapper.
- Bake uncovered at 180°C for 25 minutes or until fish flakes easily with a fork.

Tuna-Asparagus Pie

2 sheets frozen puff pastry, thawed

1 (200 g) can solid white tuna in water, drained, flaked

1 (410 g) can cut asparagus, drained

1 cup shredded cheddar cheese

- Preheat oven to 190°C.
- Line a 20 × 20 × 5 cm square cake pan with 1 sheet of puffed pastry. Spread on the tuna then the asparagus, followed by the shredded cheese.
- Cover with 2nd pastry sheet, bake about 20 minutes or until the top is golden brown and the cheese is bubbling.

Tuna Toast

1 (300 mL) can cream of chicken soup

1 (200 g) can tuna in water, drained

2 slices thick toasting bread

1 tomato, cut into chunks

- In saucepan, combine soup and tuna; stirring to break up chunks of tuna.
- Toast the bread on both sides. Pour soup mixture over toast.
- Sprinkle tomatoes over top. Serve immediately.

Tuna Noodles

1 (250 g) packet ribbon noodles, cooked, drained

2 (200 g) cans white tuna, drained

1 (300 g) can cream of chicken soup, $^{3}/_{4}$ cup milk

$^{3}/_{4}$ cup chopped black olives

- Place half the noodles in a 2 litre buttered casserole dish.
- In saucepan, combine the tuna, soup, milk and olives. Heat just enough to mix well.
- Pour half the soup mixture over noodles. Repeat layers.
- Cover and bake at 150°C for about 20 minutes.

Home Fried Fish

750 g haddock, sole or cod

1 egg, beaten

2 tablespoons milk

2 cups corn flake crumbs

- Cut fish into serving-size pieces.
- Combine egg and milk. Dip fish in egg mixture and coat with the crushed corn flakes on both sides.
- Fry in a thin layer of oil in a frying pan until brown on both sides.

Crispy Flounder

1/3 cup mayonnaise

500 g flounder fillets

1 cup seasoned breadcrumbs

1/4 cup grated parmesan cheese

- Place mayonnaise in a small dish. Coat the fish with mayonnaise and dip in crumbs to coat well.
- Arrange in a shallow baking dish. Bake uncovered at 190°C for 25 minutes.

Haddock Fillets

1 1/2 cups lemon lime soda

500 g haddock fillets

2 cups pancake batter, ready mixed

1/4 teaspoon pepper

- Pour soda in a shallow bowl; add fillets and let marinate for 15 minutes.
- In another shallow bowl combine pancake mix and pepper.
- Remove fish from soda and coat with pancake mix.
- In a large frying pan heat about 1/2 cm of oil. Fry fish for about 3 minutes on each side until fish flakes with a fork. Drain on paper towels.

Chips and Fish

1 cup mayonnaise

2 tablespoons fresh lime juice and lime wedges

3–4 fish fillets, rinsed, dried

1½ cups crushed corn chips

- Preheat oven to 210°C. Mix mayonnaise and lime juice. Spread on both sides of the fish fillets.
- Place the crushed corn chips on wax paper and dredge both sides of the fish in the chips. Shake off the excess chips.
- Place the fillets on a foil-covered baking sheet and bake for 15 minutes or until the fish flakes. Serve with lime wedges.

Red Fish Barbecue

1 kg red fish fillets

1 (250 mL) bottle Italian dressing

1 (340 g) can beer

Several dashes of Tabasco

- Place the fish in a glass casserole dish. Pour Italian dressing, beer and Tabasco over fish.
- Cover and marinate in refrigerator at least 2 hours. When ready to cook, drain the fish and place in a microwave safe container.
- Microwave fish about 4 to 5 minutes per 500 g.

Orange Roughy with Peppers

750 g orange roughy or other firm white fish

2 red capsicums, cut into julienne strips

1 teaspoon dried thyme leaves

¾ teaspoon seasoned salt

- Cut fish into serving-size pieces.
- Heat a little oil in a frying pan. Layer the capsicums and seasoning. Place fish on top.
- Turn burner on high until fish is hot enough to begin cooking.
- Lower heat, cover and cook fish for 15 to 20 minutes or until fish flakes easily.

Baked Flounder

1 kg flounder fillets (2 cm thick)

1 (300 mL) carton sour cream

$^1/_2$ cup grated parmesan cheese

$^3/_4$ teaspoon chopped dill

- Place flounder in a greased 23 × 33 cm baking dish.
- Combine the sour cream, parmesan cheese and dill; salt and pepper if desired. Spoon over flounder.
- Cover and bake at 160°C for 20 minutes.
- Uncover and sprinkle with paprika. Bake another 10 minutes longer or until fish flakes easily with a fork.

Grilled Salmon Steaks

4 ($2^1/_2$ cm thick) salmon steaks

Garlic salt

Worcestershire sauce

$^1/_4$–$^1/_2$ cup melted butter

- Place salmon steaks on baking sheet and sprinkle both sides with garlic salt.
- Splash worcestershire and butter on top of each steak and grill for 2–3 minutes.
- Remove from grill and turn each steak. Splash worcestershire and butter on top and grill for 2–3 minutes. (Do not overcook. Fish will flake, but should not be dry inside.)
- Top with a little melted butter just before serving.

Crab-Potato Salad

5 potatoes, peeled and cubed

500 g imitation crabmeat (seafood sticks), chopped

1 cup finely chopped onion

2 cups mayonnaise

- Place potatoes in a saucepan covered with water; bring to the boil and cook for about 20 minutes or until tender. Drain and cool.
- In a large bowl combine the potatoes, crabmeat, onion, salt and pepper. Toss with the mayonnaise.
- Refrigerate for about 3 hours before serving.

Baked Oysters

1 cup shucked oysters, drained, rinsed

2 cups cracker crumbs

60 g margarine, melted

½ cup milk

- Make alternate layers of oysters, cracker crumbs and margarine in a 18 × 28 cm baking dish.
- Pour warmed milk over layers adding lots of salt and pepper.
- Bake at 180°C for about 35 minutes.

Butter Fish

500 g cod or flounder fillets

120 g butter

Lemon juice

- Place butter in shallow baking dish in a very hot oven until butter is melted and slightly browned.
- Place fillets in hot butter and cook 10 minutes at 210°C.
- Turn and baste with pan juices. Sprinkle fish with lemon juice and a little salt and pepper.
- Bake another 10 minutes or until fish flakes easily.

Salmon Patties

1 (440 g) can pink salmon, reserve juice

1 egg

½ cup cracker crumbs

1 teaspoon baking powder

- Pour off juice from salmon and set aside. Remove the bones and skin.
- Stir in egg and cracker crumbs with salmon.
- In a small bowl add baking powder to ¼ cup of salmon juice. Mixture will foam. After foaming add to salmon mixture.
- Drop by teaspoons in deep hot oil in frying pan. Brown lightly on both sides. Serve hot.

Lemon Baked Fish

500 g sole or flounder fillets

30 g margarine

1 teaspoon dried tarragon

2 tablespoons lemon juice

- Place fish fillets in a greased, shallow pan. Sprinkle with salt, pepper and a little of the margarine.
- Bake at 190°C for about 8–10 minutes. Turn and bake another 6 minutes or until fish is flaky.
- Melt margarine with the tarragon and lemon juice. Serve over warm fish fillets.

DESSERTS

Peaches and Cream

1 (825 g) can sliced peaches

1 (85 g) packet peach jelly crystals

1 litre vanilla ice cream, softened

1 (310 g) can mandarin segments, drained

- Drain peaches, reserving 1 cup liquid. Cut peach slices into cubes.
- Heat peach liquid and $^1/_2$ cup water until boiling. Add jelly crystals and mix well.
- Fold in vanilla ice cream, stirring well.
- Add peaches and mandarin segments and pour into a mould, chill until set.

Ginger Dressing for Fruit Salad

1 cup vanilla yoghurt

2 tablespoons honey

1 teaspoon sugar

2 tablespoons finely chopped, crystallised ginger

- Combine all ingredients; mixing well. Cover and refrigerate. This may be served over any fruit salad.

Pear Mousse

2 (420 g) cans sliced pears, reserve juice

1 (85 g) packet lemon jelly crystals

1 (250 g) packet cream cheese, softened

1 (300 mL) carton thickened cream, whipped

- Drain pears, reserving juice. Heat juice and add water to make $^3/_4$ cup. Heat juice to boiling point. Add jelly crystals. Mix well and cool.
- Place pears and cream cheese in blender and blend until smooth. Place into a large bowl and fold in cooled but not congealed jelly mixture and whipped cream. Mix until smooth.
- Pour into individual dessert dishes. Cover with a piece of plastic wrap, refrigerate.

To garnish place a slice of kiwi fruit on top of the mousse.

Caramel-Cinnamon Dessert

1 (75 g) packet French vanilla instant pudding

3 cups milk

1 (300 mL) carton thickened cream, whipped

1 packet Nice biscuits

- Combine the pudding and milk, mixing well. Fold in whipped cream.
- Line bottom of 23 × 33 cm glass dish with whole Nice biscuits.
- Put half the pudding mixture over biscuits and top with a second layer of biscuits. Spread remaining pudding over top. Top with the remaining biscuits (you should have 2 or 3 biscuits left over from the box).
- Add a prepared caramel icing over the last layer of biscuits. Refrigerate.

Make this a day ahead of time so the pudding can soak into the biscuits.

Macaroon Delight

12 soft coconut macaroons

1 (300 mL) carton thickened cream, whipped

$1^1/_2$ litres sorbet: 1 each, orange, lime, raspberry; softened

- Warm macaroons in a 150°C oven for 10 minutes. Then break into pieces and cool.
- Spoon macaroons into the whipped cream.
- Completely line a 23 × 12 cm loaf pan with foil. First spread $^1/_2$ litre of the orange sorbet in loaf pan.
- Then spread $^1/_2$ of the whipped cream mixture, next the lime sorbet and the remaining whipped cream mixture. Raspberry sorbet will be on top.
- Freeze overnight. To serve unmould and remove foil and slice.

Caramel-Apple Delight

4 (60 g) Snickers candy bars, frozen

2 Granny Smith apples, chopped

1 (600 mL) carton thickened cream, whipped

1 (100 g) packet dry instant vanilla pudding

- Smash frozen candy bars in the wrappers with a hammer.
- Mix all ingredients together.
- Refrigerate.

Place in a pretty crystal bowl or serve in individual sorbet glasses.

Coffee Mallow

3 cups miniature marshmallows

½ cup hot, strong coffee

1 cup thickened cream, whipped

½ teaspoon vanilla

- In a large saucepan, combine marshmallows and coffee. On low heat and stirring constantly, cook until marshmallows have melted. Cool this mixture.
- Fold in whipped cream and vanilla.
- Pour into individual dessert glasses. Stir until ready to serve.

Grape Fluff

1 cup grape juice

2 cups miniature marshmallows

2 tablespoons lemon juice

1 (300 mL) carton thickened cream, whipped

- In saucepan, heat grape juice to boiling. Add marshmallows. Stir constantly until melted.
- Add lemon juice and cool.
- Fold in whipped cream and spoon into individual serving dishes. Refrigerate.

Apricot Pudding

1 (100 g) packet vanilla pudding (not instant)

1 (425 g) can apricot halves, reserve juice

1 (310 g) can mandarin oranges, drained

1 (300 mL) carton thickened cream, whipped

- Cook pudding with $1^1/_4$ cups apricot juice (adding water to make the $1^1/_4$ cups). Cool.
- Add drained oranges and cut-up apricots. Refrigerate until mixture begins to thicken.
- Fold in whipped cream. Spoon into 6 individual sorbet dishes.

Peachy Sundaes

$^1/_2$ litre vanilla ice cream

$^3/_4$ cup chunky peach jam, warmed

$^1/_4$ cup chopped almonds, toasted

$^1/_4$ cup coconut

- Divide ice cream into 4 sorbet dishes.
- Top with peach jam.
- Sprinkle with almonds and coconut.

Mango Cream

2 soft mangoes

2 litres vanilla ice cream, softened

$^1/_4$ cup lemon juice

1 (300 mL) carton thickened cream, whipped

- Peel the mangoes and cut slices around the seed; then cut into small chunks.
- In a large bowl, mix together the ice cream, lemon juice and whipped cream.
- Fold in the mango chunks.
- Quickly spoon mixture into parfait glasses or sorbets; cover with plastic wrap. Place in freezer until firm.

Cookies and Cream

25 chocolate chip cookies, crushed

2 litres vanilla ice cream, softened

150 mL chocolate syrup

1 (300 mL) carton thickened cream, whipped

- Press crushed cookies in a 23 × 33 cm baking dish. Spread ice cream over cookies.
- Pour syrup over the ice cream and top with the whipped cream.
- Freeze overnight.
- Slice into squares to serve.

Peanut Butter Sundae

1 cup light corn syrup

1 cup chunky peanut butter

$^1/_4$ cup milk

Ice cream or plain cake to serve

- In a mixing bowl, stir together the corn syrup, peanut butter and milk until well blended.
- Serve over ice cream or plain cake. Store in refrigerator.

Strawberry Trifle

1 (100 g) packet French vanilla instant pudding mix

1 (300 g) frozen loaf plain cake, thawed

$^1/_2$ cup sherry

1 punnet fresh strawberries

- Make pudding as instructed on packet.
- Place a layer of plain cake slices in the bottom of a 20 cm crystal bowl. Sprinkle with $^1/_4$ cup of the sherry. Add a layer of strawberries. Next, add a layer of half the pudding. Repeat these layers. Refrigerate overnight or several hours.
- Before serving, top with whipped cream.

Amaretto Ice Cream

1 (300 g) carton thickened cream, whipped

500 mL vanilla ice cream, softened

$^1/_3$ cup amaretto

$^1/_3$ cup chopped almonds, toasted

- Combine whipped cream, ice cream and amaretto. Freeze in sorbet glasses.
- When ready to serve, drizzle a little additional amaretto over the top of each individual serving and sprinkle with toasted almonds.

You can make your own amaretto by following the recipe for amaretto on page 62. It's great.

Blueberry Fluff

1 (425 g) can blueberries, drained and mashed with 2 tablespoons sugar

1 (440 g) can crushed pineapple, drained

1 (395 g) sweetened condensed milk

1 (300 mL) carton thickened cream, whipped

- Mix mashed blueberries, pineapple and condensed milk together.
- Fold in whipped cream. (This dessert is even better if you add $^3/_4$ cup of chopped pecans.)
- Combine all ingredients and pour into parfait glasses. Refrigerate.

Winter Wonder Dessert

1 (250 g) packet chocolate cream-filled chocolate biscuits, divided

$2^3/_4$ cups milk

3 (100 g) packets instant strawberry pudding

1 (300 mL) carton thickened cream, whipped

- Crush the cookies, reserving $^2/_3$ of a cup. Place crushed cookies in a 23 × 33 cm dish.
- In a mixing bowl, combine milk and instant pudding. Mix about 2 minutes until thickened. Pour over crushed cookies.
- Spread whipped cream over strawberry pudding.
- Sprinkle the reserved cookies over the top of whipped cream and refrigerate overnight before serving.

Divine Strawberries

2 punnets fresh strawberries

1 (440 g) can pineapple pieces, well drained

2 bananas, sliced

1 (500 g) bottle strawberry topping

- Cut strawberries in half (or in quarters if the strawberries are very large).
- Add pineapple pieces and bananas.
- Fold in the strawberry topping and chill.

This is wonderful served over plain cake or just served in sorbet glasses.

Amaretto Peaches

$4^1/_2$ cups peeled, sliced fresh peaches

$^1/_2$ cup amaretto

$^1/_2$ cup sour cream

$^1/_2$ cup packed brown sugar

- Lay the peaches in a 2 litre baking dish. Pour amaretto over peaches and spread sour cream over peaches. Sprinkle brown sugar evenly over all.
- Grill mixture until it is heated thoroughly and sugar melts.

Serve over ice cream or plain cake.

Brandied Apples

1 (300 g) frozen loaf plain cake, thawed

1 (450 g) can apple pie filling

$^1/_2$ teaspoon allspice

2 tablespoons brandy

- Slice plain cake and place on dessert plates.
- In a saucepan, combine pie filling, allspice and brandy. Heat and stir just until heated thoroughly.
- Place several spoonfuls over cake. Top with a scoop of vanilla ice cream.

Amaretto Sauce for Plain Cake

1 (95 g) packet French vanilla pudding (not instant)

1 cup milk

1 (300 mL) carton thickened cream, whipped

$^1/_4$ cup amaretto

- Cook pudding with the milk according to packet directions. Cover and cool to room temperature.
- With a wire whisk, stir in whipped cream and amaretto.
- Pour over plain cake or vanilla ice cream.

Boiled Custard

1 (395 g) can sweetened condensed milk

1 litre milk

5 eggs

$^1/_2$ teaspoon vanilla

- Combine the milk and heat in the top of a double boiler.
- In a separate pan, beat the eggs well.
- Slowly pour a little of the milk over the eggs, stirring constantly. Gradually add the eggs to the milk and cook on low for 5 to 10 minutes, stirring constantly, until thickened.
- Stir in vanilla and refrigerate.

This can be served in custard cups or stemmed glasses.

Chocolate-Coconut Mist

800 g flaked coconut

2 tablespoons butter, optional

$1^1/_3$ cups semi-sweet chocolate chips, melted

2 litres mint chocolate chip ice cream

- In a bowl, toss coconut, butter and chocolate together until well blended.
- On a baking sheet covered with waxed paper, shape about $^1/_3$ cupfuls into 6 cm nests. Chill until firm.

Just before serving top each nest with $^1/_2$ cup of ice cream.

Butterscotch Finale

1 (600 mL) carton thickened cream

$^3/_4$ cup butterscotch topping

1 (24 cm diameter) sponge cake

340 g toffee bars, crushed, divided

- In a mixer bowl, whip the cream until it begins to thicken.
- Slowly add butterscotch topping and continue beating until mixture is thick.
- Slice cake into 3 equal horizontal layers.
- With bottom layer on a cake plate, spread with about $1^1/_2$ cups of the whipped cream mixture. Sprinkle with $^1/_4$ of the crushed toffee.
- Repeat layers and frost top as well as sides of the cake.
- Sprinkle toffee over top of cake. Refrigerate at least 8 hours before serving.

Black Forest Cake

1 rich chocolate cake mix

1 (680 g) can pitted cherries, drained and mashed with 1 tablespoon sugar

1 (100 g) packet vanilla instant pudding

1 (300 mL) carton thickened cream, whipped

- Bake cake according to directions in a greased and floured 23 × 33 cm baking pan.
- While cake is still warm poke top with fork and spread mashed cherries over cake.
- While cake cools, prepare the pudding using 1 cup of milk. Fold in the whipped cream.
- Spread pudding and whipped cream mixture over cake, carefully covering the mashed cherries. Refrigerate.

Pecan Cake

1 butter cake mix

120 g margarine, melted

1 egg

1 cup chopped pecans

- Combine cake mix, $^3/_4$ cup water, margarine and egg, mixing well. Stir in pecans.
- Pour into a 23 × 33 cm baking dish.

Topping for Pecan Cake

1 (250 g) packet cream cheese, softened

2 eggs

450 g icing sugar

- With a mixer, combine cream cheese, eggs and icing sugar. Pour over cake mixture.
- Bake at 180°C for 40 minutes. Check with skewer to make sure cake is done.

Oreo Cake

1 packet white cake mix

1/3 cup oil

4 egg whites

1 1/4 cups coarsely chopped Oreo cookies

- In a mixer bowl combine cake mix, oil, 1 1/4 cups water and egg whites. Blend on low speed until moistened. Then beat 2 minutes at high speed.
- Gently fold in coarsely chopped cookies. Pour batter into two greased and floured 20 cm round cake pans.
- Bake at 180°C for 25 to 30 minutes or until skewer inserted in centre comes out clean.
- Cool for 15 minutes; then remove from pan. Let cool completely and frost.

Frosting for Oreo Cake

4 1/4 cups icing sugar

125 g butter, softened

250 g margarine shortening (not butter flavoured)

1 teaspoon almond flavouring

- With a mixer combine all ingredients. Beat together until creamy.
- Ice the first layer of cake and place second layer on top; ice top and sides.
- Sprinkle with extra crushed Oreo cookies on top.

Favourite Cake

1 butter cake mix

1 cup almond or peanut brittle toffee, broken into bits

1 cup chopped pecans

Icing sugar

- Mix cake mix according to packet directions. Fold in toffee bits and pecans.
- Pour into a greased and floured tube cake pan. Bake at 180°C for 45 minutes or until skewer inserted in centre comes out clean.
- Allow cake to cool several minutes; then remove cake from pan. Dust with sifted icing sugar.

Delightful Pear Cake

1 (425 g) can pears in light syrup, undrained

1 vanilla cake mix

2 egg whites

1 whole egg

- Drain pears, reserving the liquid; chop pears.
- Place pears and the liquid in a mixing bowl; add cake mix, egg whites and whole egg. Beat on low speed for 30 seconds. Beat on high for 4 minutes.
- Grease and flour a 26 cm tube pan. Pour in batter.
- Bake at 180°C for 50 to 55 minutes. Cook until a skewer inserted in middle comes out clean. Cool in pan for about 10 minutes. Remove cake and dust with sifted icing sugar.

Miracle Cake

1 vanilla cake mix

1 teaspoon grated lemon rind

3 eggs

1 (450 g) can crushed pineapple, undrained

- In a mixing bowl combine all ingredients with $^1/_3$ cup oil.
- Blend on low speed; then beat on medium for 2 minutes.
- Pour batter into a greased and floured 23 × 33 cm baking dish.
- Bake for 30 to 35 minutes until cake tests done with a skewer. Cool and top with Miracle Cake Topping.

Miracle Cake Topping

1 (395 g) can sweetened condensed milk

$^1/_4$ cup lemon juice

$1^1/_2$ cups whipped cream

- Blend all ingredients, mixing well. Spread over cake. Refrigerate.

Chocolate Pudding Cake

1 milk chocolate cake mix

$1^1/_4$ cups milk

$^1/_3$ cup oil

3 eggs

- In a mixing bowl combine all ingredients. Beat well.
- Pour into a greased and buttered 23 × 33 cm baking pan.
- Bake at 180°C for 35 minutes or skewer comes out clean.

Frosting for Chocolate Pudding Cake

1 (395 g) can sweetened condensed milk

1 cup chocolate syrup

$1^1/_2$ cups whipped cream

$^1/_3$ cup chopped pecans

- In a small bowl mix the sweetened condensed milk and chocolate syrup.
- Pour over cake and let soak into cake. Chill for several hours.
- Spread whipped cream over top of cake and sprinkle pecans over the top. Refrigerate.

O'Shaughnessy's Special

1 (300 g) plain cake loaf

$^2/_3$ (825 g) can crushed pineapple, undrained

1 (100 g) packet vanilla instant pudding mix

$1^1/_2$ cups whipped cream

- Slice cake horizontally, making 3 layers.
- Combine pineapple and pudding; beat until mixture begins to thicken; fold in whipped cream, blending well. (Add a few drops of green food colouring if you like.)
- Spread on each layer and on top. Refrigerate.

Carnival Cake

1 vanilla cake mix

2 (300 g) boxes frozen strawberries, thawed

1 (100 g) packet instant vanilla pudding

1 (300 mL) carton thickened cream, whipped

- Make cake mix by following directions on packet. Pour into a greased 23 × 33 cm baking dish. Bake according to packet directions.
- When cool, poke holes with a knife in the top of the cake and pour strawberries over the top of the cake.
- Make up the packet of instant pudding using $1^1/_4$ cups milk and when that is set, pour over the strawberries. Cover cake with the whipped cream. Refrigerate.

Chocolate-Cherry Cake

1 chocolate cake mix

1 (410 g) can cherries, drained and chopped

3 eggs

- In a mixing bowl, combine all ingredients. Mix by hand.
- Pour into a greased and floured 23 × 33 cm baking dish.
- Bake at 180°C for 35 to 40 minutes. Test with skewer for doneness.

Chocolate-Cherry Cake Frosting

75 g butter

$1^1/_4$ cups sugar

$^1/_2$ cup milk

170 g chocolate chips

- When cake is done, combine margarine, sugar and milk in a medium saucepan. Boil 1 minute, stirring constantly. Add chocolate chips and stir until chips are melted. Pour over hot cake.

Hawaiian Dream Cake

1 yellow cake mix

4 eggs

$^3/_4$ cup oil

$^1/_2$ (440 g) can crushed pineapple with $^1/_2$ juice

- With mixer beat together all ingredients for 4 minutes.
- Pour into a greased and floured 23 × 33 cm baking pan.
- Bake at 180°C for 30 to 35 minutes or until cake tests done with skewer. Cool.

Coconut-Pineapple Icing for Hawaiian Dream Cake

$^1/_2$ (440 g) can crushed pineapple with $^1/_2$ juice

120 g margarine

1 (500 g) packet icing sugar

200 g coconut

- Heat together the pineapple and margarine. Boil $1^1/_2$ minutes.
- Add icing sugar and coconut.
- Punch holes in cake with knife. Pour hot icing over cake.

Plain Cake Deluxe

1 (25 cm) round bakery plain cake (buttercake)

1 (440 g) can crushed pineapple, undrained

1 (100 g) packet vanilla instant pudding mix

1 (300 mL) carton thickened cream, whipped

- Slice cake horizontally to make 3 layers.
- Mix pineapple, pudding mix and whipped cream together, blending well.
- Spread on each layer and top of cake. Coconut can be sprinkled on top layer. Refrigerate.

Fluffy Orange Cake

1 vanilla cake mix

4 eggs

$^2/_3$ cup oil

$^1/_2$ cup orange juice

- In a mixer bowl, combine all ingredients.
- Beat on low speed to blend then beat on medium speed for 2 minutes. Pour into a greased and floured 23 × 33 cm baking pan.
- Bake at 180°C for 30 minutes or until cake test is done. Cool.

Topping for Fluffy Orange Cake

1 (395 g) can sweetened condensed milk

$^1/_3$ cup lemon juice

1 (300 mL) carton thickened cream, whipped

2 (310 g) cans mandarin orange segments, drained, cut in half, chilled

- In a large bowl blend condensed milk and lemon juice, mixing well.
- Fold in whipped cream until blended. Fold in orange segments.
- Pour mixture over cooled cake. Cover and refrigerate.

Basic Pound Cake

360 g butter

3 cups sugar

8 eggs

3 cups sifted flour

- In a mixer, cream together butter and sugar, mixing well.
- Add eggs one at a time, beating well after each addition. Add flour, stirring in small amounts at a time.
- Pour into a greased and floured 25 cm tube pan and bake at 150°C for $1^1/_2$ hours.

Do not open oven door during baking.

Emergency Cheesecake

1 (250 g) packet cream cheese, softened

1 (395 g) can sweetened condensed milk

$^1/_2$ cup lemon juice

1 teaspoon vanilla

- Blend all ingredients in mixer.
- Pour into a biscuit crumb pie crust. Refigerate.

To serve, top with 1 cup canned cherries.

Chiffon Torte

1 slab or round bakery sponge cake

1 (440 g) can crushed pineapple, undrained

1 (100 g) packet vanilla instant pudding

1 (300 mL) carton thickened cream, whipped

- Slice cake horizontally to make 3 layers.
- In a bowl, combine pineapple and pudding, beat by hand until mixture begins to thicken. Fold in whipped cream.
- Spread on each layer and cover top of cake.
- Refrigerate overnight.

Toasted almonds can be sprinkled on top of cake.

Chocolate-Orange Cake

1 (300 g) loaf frozen plain cake, thawed

1 (250 g) jar orange marmalade

1 (450 g) can ready-to-spread chocolate fudge frosting

- Cut cake horizontally to make 3 layers.
- Place one layer on cake platter. Spread with half of the marmalade.
- Place second layer over first and spread on remaining marmalade.
- Top with third cake layer and spread frosting liberally on top and sides of cake. Refrigerate.

Easy Pineapple Cake

1$^3/_4$ cups sugar

1$^3/_4$ cups flour

1 (440 g) can crushed pineapple, undrained

1 teaspoon baking soda

- Combine all ingredients and mix by hand.
- Pour into a greased and floured 23 × 33 cm baking pan.
- Bake at 180°C for 30 to 35 minutes.

Icing for Easy Pineapple Cake

1 (250 g) packet cream cheese, softened

120 g margarine, melted

1 cup icing sugar

1 cup chopped pecans

- Combine cream cheese, margarine and icing sugar and beat with mixer.
- Add the chopped pecans and pour over HOT cake.

Strawberry Delight

1 (200 g) packet strawberry jelly crystals

2 (300 g) packets frozen strawberries, undrained

1 (300 mL) carton thickened cream, whipped

1 (340 g) prepared sponge cake

- Dissolve strawberry jelly crystals in 1 cup boiling water; mixing well. Add strawberries.
- Chill in refrigerator until partially set.
- Fold in whipped cream.
- Break the sponge cake into large bite-size pieces and layer the cake and jelly mixture half at a time in a 23 × 33 cm shallow dish. Refrigerate.

Cut in squares to serve.

Angel Glaze

1 cup icing sugar

1 tablespoon hot water

2 tablespoons light corn syrup

¼ teaspoon vanilla

- Mix all ingredients and stir until well blended with creamy texture. Glaze should pour slowly and stay on cake long enough to soak in. If glaze runs down the side of the cake, thicken the mixture with a little more icing sugar.
- Use on any cake that needs a light icing or a topping of something sweet.

Chocolate-Amaretto Pie

2 (200 g) milk chocolate almond candy bars

$^1/_3$ cup amaretto

2 (300 mL) cartons thickened cream, whipped

1 (23 cm) shortcrust pie crust

- Melt chocolate in double boiler on low heat. Remove from heat and pour in amaretto.
- Stir chocolate and amaretto for about 10 or 15 minutes until mixture is room temperature.
- Fold in whipped cream.
- Pour into pie crust. Chill several hours before serving.

Creamy Cherry-Apricot Pie

2 (200 g) cartons apricot yoghurt

$^1/_2$ cup chopped maraschino cherries, divided

1 (300 mL) carton thickened cream, whipped

1 (23 cm) biscuit crumb pie crust

- Stir together the yoghurt and $^1/_4$ cup cherries.
- Fold in whipped cream.
- Spoon the mixture into the pie crust and garnish with chopped cherries.
- Refrigerate 6–8 hours or until firm.

Magic Cherry Pie

2 (200 g) cartons cherry yoghurt

1 (85 g) packet dry cherry jelly crystals

1 (300 mL) carton thickened cream, whipped

1 shortcrust pie crust

- In a bowl, combine the yoghurt and dry jelly crystals, mixing well.
- Fold in the whipped cream and spoon into pie crust.
- Freeze. Take out of freezer 20 minutes before slicing.

You could also place a dab of cherry syrup on top of pie which will make it even better.

Cool Chocolate Pie

22 large marshmallows

2 (250 g) milk chocolate almond candy bars

1 (300 mL) carton thickened cream, whipped

$^{1}/_{2}$ cup chopped pecans

- In a double boiler, melt marshmallows and chocolate bars.
- Cool partially and fold in whipped cream and pecans.
- Pour into a prepared biscuit crumb pie crust.
- Refrigerate several hours before serving.

Creamy Lime-Almond Pie

1 (200 g) packet biscuit crumbs

$^{1}/_{3}$ cup melted margarine or butter

1 cup lime sorbet, softened

1 cup whipped cream

- Preheat oven to 180°C. Mix $1^{1}/_{2}$ cups biscuit crumbs with margarine and pat evenly into a 23 cm pie plate.
- Bake 10 minutes, remove and cool.
- Fold together the sorbet and whipped cream. Place in the crumb crust and sprinkle $^{1}/_{2}$ cup biscuit crumbs on top.
- Refrigerate 6–8 hours or until firm.

Strawberry Pie

2 (85 g) packets strawberry jelly crystals

1 cup boiling water

1 (300 mL) carton thickened cream, whipped

2 punnets fresh strawberries, chopped

- In a bowl, combine jelly crystals and boiling water, mixing well. Let jelly cool in the refrigerator until it begins to thicken. (Watch closely.)
- Fold in whipped cream and strawberries.
- Spoon into a biscuit crumb pie crust.
- Refrigerate several hours before serving.

Million Dollar Pie

24 Ritz crackers, crumbled

1 cup chopped pecans

4 egg whites (absolutely no yolks at all)

1 cup sugar

- Mix cracker crumbs with pecans.
- In a separate mixing bowl, beat egg whites until stiff; slowly add sugar while still mixing.
- Gently fold in the crumbs and pecan mixture into egg whites. Pour into a pie tin and bake at 180°C for 20 minutes. Cool before serving.

Top with a scoop of chocolate ice cream.

Very Berry Pie

2 (85 g) packets strawberry jelly crystals

2 (275 g) jars cranberry sauce

2 cups whipped cream

- Dissolve jelly crystals in $^{3}/_{4}$ cup boiling water.
- Add cranberry sauce. Place in refrigerator until it begins to thicken.
- Fold in whipped cream and pour into a 23 cm biscuit crumb pie crust. Refrigerate for 3 hours.

Apricot Pie

2 (440 g) cans apricot halves, drained

1$^{1}/_{4}$ cups sugar

$^{1}/_{4}$ cup flour

1 (300 mL) carton thickened cream

- Cut each apricot half in half and arrange evenly in an unbaked 28 cm pie shell.
- Combine sugar and flour and sprinkle over apricots.
- Pour unwhipped cream over pie.
- Place 2$^{1}/_{2}$-cm strips of foil over edge of pie crust to keep from browning too much. Bake at 160°C for 1 hour 20 minutes.

You might want to place the pie on a baking sheet to catch any spillovers.

Caramel Ice Cream Pie

1 packet scotch finger biscuits

2 litres vanilla ice cream

3/4 (500 mL) bottle caramel sauce

- Roughly crumble the biscuits and place in a 25 cm pie plate keeping out about 1/2 cup to use for topping.
- Place ice cream in a bowl to soften. Stir caramel sauce into the ice cream (do not mix completely) and spoon mixture into the pie plate.
- Sprinkle remaining biscuit crumbs over top of pie. Freeze.

Pineapple Fluff Pie

1 (440 g) can crushed pineapple, undrained

1 (100 g) packet instant vanilla pudding mix

1 (300 mL) carton thickened cream, whipped

1 (23 cm) biscuit crumb pie crust

- In a bowl, combine the pineapple and pudding mix; beat until thickened.
- Fold in the whipped cream.
- Spoon into pie crust.
- Refrigerate several hours before serving.

Chocolate-Vanilla-Almond Parfait

1 (100 g) packet instant chocolate pudding mix

1 (100 g) packet instant vanilla pudding mix

4 cups milk

2 cups slivered almonds

- Using 2 mixing bowls, prepare each pudding with milk as directed. Cover tightly with plastic wrap and refrigerate.
- Place slivered almonds in a dry frying pan over medium heat. Stir until almonds are evenly browned.
- In parfait glasses or stemmed glasses, first spoon small amounts of chocolate pudding, then vanilla pudding to the top of the glass. Garnish with almonds. Refrigerate until chilled.

Apricot Chiffon Pie

2 (200 g) cartons apricot-mango yoghurt

1 (85 g) packet apricot jelly crystals

1 (300 mL) carton thickened cream, whipped

1 medium size frozen flan base, thawed

- In a bowl, combine yoghurt and jelly crystals, mixing well.
- Fold in whipped cream and spread in flan base. Freeze.
- Take out of freezer 20 minutes before slicing.

Holiday Pie

1 (250 g) packet cream cheese, softened

1 (395 g) can sweetened condensed milk

1 (100 g) packet instant vanilla pudding mix

1½ cups whipped cream

- With a mixer, beat cream cheese until smooth. Gradually add sweetened condensed milk and beat until smooth.
- Add ¾ cup water and the pudding mix; beat until smooth.
- Fold in whipped cream.
- Pour into a biscuit crumb pie shell. Top with grated chocolate.

Peaches 'N Cream Pie

Chocolate syrup

1 litre peach ice cream, softened

Fresh peach slices

¼ cup pecan halves

- Drizzle ½ cup chocolate syrup over the bottom of a prepared shortcrust pie shell.
- Spoon ice cream over crust and freeze for 3 hours or until firm.
- When ready to serve, place peach slices and pecan halves over top of ice cream.
- Drizzle with additional chocolate syrup.

Banana Split Pie

3 small bananas

1 litre vanilla ice cream, softened

Fudge sauce

1 (300 mL) carton thickened cream, whipped

- Slice bananas and place in a crumb crust pie shell.
- Spoon softened ice cream over bananas. Freeze for 2 to 3 hours.
- Spread some fudge sauce over the ice cream and top with a layer of whipped cream.
- When ready to serve, place a maraschino cherry on top of each piece of pie.

Mint-Chocolate Pie

1 cup mint-chocolate chip ice cream, softened

1 cup whipped cream

3/4 cup crushed chocolate sandwich cookies with mint filling, divided

1 (23 cm) chocolate cookie pie crust

- Fold together ice cream, whipped cream and 1/2 cup crushed cookies.
- Place in pie crust and sprinkle remaining cookie crumbs on top.
- Refrigerate 6–8 hours or until firm.

Grasshopper Pie

22 large marshmallows

1/3 cup creme de menthe

1 (300 mL) carton thickened cream, whipped

1 (23 cm) prepared chocolate pie crust

- In a large saucepan, melt marshmallows with the creme de menthe over low heat. Cool.
- Fold the whipped cream into the marshmallow mixture.
- Pour filling into pie crust and freeze until ready to serve.

Peach Crunch

2 (825 g) cans peach slices, drained

1 packet buttercake cake mix

1 cup slivered almonds

120 g margarine

- Add peach slices evenly in the bottom of a greased and floured 23 × 33 cm baking pan.
- Sprinkle cake mix evenly and smooth over top. Sprinkle almonds evenly over cake mix.
- Slice margarine into 4 mm slices and place over entire surface.
- Bake at 180°C for 40 to 45 minutes or until top is nicely browned.

Blueberry Cobbler

2 (300 g) packets frozen blueberries, thawed

1 packet vanilla cake mix

1 egg

120 g margarine, softened

- Spread blueberries in a greased 23 × 33 cm baking dish. Sprinkle lightly with sugar.
- With mixer, combine cake mix, egg and margarine. Blend well. Mixture will be stiff.
- Spoon over filling.
- Bake at 180°C for 45 minutes or until golden brown.

Cherry Cobbler

1 (750 g) can pitted cherries, drained

1 packet vanilla cake mix

180 g margarine, melted

1 (115 g) packet slivered almonds

- Spread drained cherries in a greased 23 × 33 cm baking pan and sprinkle with a little sugar.
- Sprinkle cake mix over the cherries.
- Drizzle melted margarine over top. Sprinkle almonds over the top.
- Bake at 180°C for 45 minutes. Top with whipped cream.

Cream Cheese Crust

120 g margarine, softened

85 g cream cheese, softened

1 cup flour

- Combine margarine, cream cheese and flour.
- Blend with a pastry blender or with a fork until mixture can be made into a ball.
- Chill pastry for about 1 hour.
- Roll out on a floured surface.

Makes one 23 cm crust.

Cherry Crisp

1 (750 g) can pitted cherries, drained

1 packet vanilla cake mix

120 g margarine

2 cups chopped pecans

- Pour drained cherries into a greased 23 × 33 cm baking dish.
- Sprinkle cake mix over top of cherries.
- Dot with margarine and cover with pecans.
- Bake uncovered at 180°C for 45 minutes.

Easy Chocolate Pie

1 frozen pie crust, cooked

1 (600 mL) carton thickened cream, whipped, divided

250 g milk chocolate bar

3/4 cup chopped pecans

- In a saucepan, break chocolate into small pieces and melt over low heat.
- Remove and let set several minutes until cooled to blood heat.
- Fold in 2/3 of the whipped cream, mixing well.
- Stir in chopped pecans and pour into pie crust.
- Spread remaining whipped cream over top of pie. Refrigerate at least 8 hours.

Butter Cookie Special

1 packet butter cake mix

1 (85 g) packet vanilla instant pudding mix

1 cup oil

1 egg, beaten

1¼ cups chopped pecans

- Mixing by hand stir together cake mix, pudding mix, oil and egg. Beat thoroughly.
- Stir in pecans. With a teaspoon drop cookie dough onto baking tray about 5 cm apart.
- Bake at 180°C for about 8 minutes. Do not overcook.

Coconut Macaroons

2 (170 g) packets flaked coconut

1 (395 g) can condensed milk

2 teaspoons vanilla

½ teaspoon almond extract

- In a mixing bowl combine coconut, condensed milk and extracts; mix well.
- Line a baking tray with foil and grease the foil. Drop by rounded teaspoons onto baking tray.
- Bake at 180°C for 8 to 10 minutes or until lightly browned around edges. Immediately remove from foil. (Macaroons will stick if allowed to cool.) Store at room temperature.

Chocolate Crunch Cookies

1 packet rich chocolate cake mix

1 egg, lightly beaten

120 g margarine, melted

1 cup crisp rice bubble cereal

- Combine cake mix, egg and margarine. Add cereal; stir until blended.
- Shape dough into 2 cm balls. Place on lightly greased baking sheet.
- Dip a fork in flour and flatten cookies in a crisscross pattern. Bake at 180°C for 10 to 12 minutes. Cool.

Light Pecan Cookies

6 egg whites

3 cups icing sugar

$^{1}/_{4}$ cup cocoa

$3^{1}/_{2}$ cups finely chopped pecans

- Beat egg whites until light and frothy. Fold sugar and cocoa into egg whites and beat lightly. Fold in pecans.
- Drop by teaspoons onto a lightly greased and floured baking tray.
- Bake at 160°C for about 20 minutes. Do not overbake and cool completely before removing from tray.

Lemon Cookies

120 g butter, softened

1 cup sugar

2 tablespoons lemon juice

2 cups flour

- Cream butter, sugar and lemon juice slowly stirring in flour.
- Drop by teaspoons onto ungreased baking tray.
- Bake at 180°C for 14 to 15 minutes.

Coconut Moments

250 g margarine or butter, softened

$^{1}/_{2}$ cup icing sugar

$^{1}/_{2}$ cup cornflour, $1^{1}/_{3}$ cups flour

Flaked coconut

- Beat margarine or butter and icing sugar until light and fluffy. Add cornflour and flour; beat until well blended. Cover and refrigerate for 1 hour.
- Remove and shape into $2^{1}/_{2}$-cm balls. Roll in flaked coconut. Place on ungreased baking tray.
- Bake at 160°C for 12 to 15 minutes. Watch closely and don't let the coconut burn. Cool 2 or 3 minutes before removing from tray.

Drop Cookies

250 g margarine, softened

$^{3}/_{4}$ cup cornflour

$^{1}/_{3}$ cup icing sugar

1 cup flour

- Mix together the margarine, cornflour, sugar and flour, mixing well.
- Drop onto baking tray in small balls and flatten slightly.
- Bake at 180°C for about 15 minutes; do not brown. When cool, ice.

Icing for Drop Cookies

85 g cream cheese, softened

1 teaspoon vanilla

1 cup icing sugar

- Blend all ingredients together, mixing well. Ice cookies.

Lemon-Coconut Macaroons

$^{2}/_{3}$ cup sweetened condensed milk

1 large egg white

2 teaspoons lemon juice and 1 teaspoon lemon zest

$3^{1}/_{2}$ cups shredded or flaked coconut

- Preheat oven to 160°C. Mix condensed milk, egg white, lemon juice and lemon zest and stir in coconut.
- Drop by teaspoons, 5 cm apart, on a baking tray covered with waxed paper or foil.
- Bake 20 minutes or until lightly browned. Cool completely and remove carefully from the foil or waxed paper.

Cheesecake Cookies

1 cup butter, softened

170 g cream cheese, softened

2 cups sugar

2 cups flour

- Cream together the butter and cream cheese. Add sugar, beating until light and fluffy. Add flour, beating well.
- Drop by teaspoons onto baking tray and bake at 180°C for 12 to 15 minutes or until edges are golden.

These are made even better if you add 1 cup of chopped pecans.

Gingerbread Cookies

180 g margarine, softened

2 egg yolks

1 butter cake mix

1 teaspoon ginger and 1/2 teaspoon mixed spices

- In a large bowl combine margarine and egg yolks. Gradually blend in cake mix, ginger and mixed spices, mixing well.
- Roll out to a 4 mm thickness on a lightly floured surface. Using your gingerbread cookie cutter, cut out your cookies and place 5 cm apart on baking tray.
- Bake at 190°C for about 8 minutes or until edges are slightly browned. Cool cookies on the tray before transferring cookies to a cookie bowl.

Devil's Food Cookies

1 packet devil's food or rich chocolate cake mix

1/2 cup oil

2 eggs

3/4 cup chopped pecans, optional

- Combine the cake mix, oil and eggs in a mixer bowl; mixing well.
- Drop by teaspoons onto a non-stick baking tray.
- Bake at 180°C for 10 to 12 minutes. Cool and remove to a wire rack.

Nutty Fudgies

1 packet vanilla cake mix

1 (300 mL) carton sour cream

$^{2}/_{3}$ cup peanut brittle chips

$^{1}/_{2}$ cup chopped peanuts

- Beat cake mix and sour cream until well blended and mixture is smooth. Stir in peanut brittle chips and peanuts.
- Drop by teaspoonfuls onto a greased baking tray. Bake at 180°C for 10 to 12 minutes. Remove from oven and cool.

Chocolate-Peanut Butter Crisps

1 (10 count) packet 20 cm flour tortillas

1 (250 g) block semi-sweet chocolate, coarsely chopped or 250 g semi-sweet choc bits

$^{1}/_{3}$ cup creamy or chunky peanut butter

1 (395 g) can sweetened condensed milk

- Cut the flour tortillas into 8 wedges and place on baking tray. Bake at 180°C for 10 minutes and cool on rack.
- In a heavy saucepan, melt the chocolate over low heat, stirring constantly. Stir in the peanut butter, sweetened condensed milk and 2 tablespoons water and heat through. (If the sauce is too thick, add 1 teaspoon water at a time, until the sauce smoothly drizzles on foil.)
- Drizzle warm chocolate sauce over the wedges or serve immediately in a chafing dish (candelburner) or fondue pot and dip crisp tortilla wedges.

Peanut Butter Cookies

1 cup sugar

$^{3}/_{4}$ cup light corn syrup

1 (450 g) jar crunchy peanut butter

4$^{1}/_{2}$ cups chow mein noodles

- In a saucepan over medium heat bring sugar and corn syrup to the boil; stir in peanut butter.
- Remove from heat. Stir in noodles.
- Drop by spoonfuls onto waxed paper and allow to cool.

Butter Cookies

450 g butter (not margarine)

$^{3}/_{4}$ cup brown sugar

$^{3}/_{4}$ cup granulated sugar

$4^{1}/_{2}$ cups flour

- Cream butter and sugars together and slowly add flour, mixing well. Batter will be very thick.
- Roll into small balls and place on an ungreased baking tray.
- Bake at 180°C for about 15 minutes until only slightly brown. Do not overbake.

Butterscotch Cookies

1 (375 g) and 1 (200 g) packet butterscotch chips

$2^{1}/_{4}$ cups chow mein noodles

$^{1}/_{2}$ cup chopped walnuts

$^{1}/_{4}$ cup coconut

- Melt butterscotch chips in double boiler. Add noodles, walnuts and coconut.
- Drop by tablespoonfuls onto waxed paper.

Pecan Puffs

2 egg whites

$^{1}/_{2}$ cup packed light brown sugar

1 teaspoon vanilla

1 cup chopped pecans

- Beat egg whites until foamy. Gradually add ($^{1}/_{4}$ cup at a time) brown sugar and vanilla. Continue beating until stiff peaks are formed (about 3 or 4 minutes). Fold in pecans.
- Line a baking tray with baking paper. Drop by teaspoons onto paper.
- Bake at 100°C for 45 minutes.

Scotch Shortbread

120 g unsalted, butter, softened

$^{1}/_{3}$ cup sugar

$1^{1}/_{4}$ cups flour

Icing sugar

- Cream butter and sugar until light and fluffy. Add flour and pinch of salt, mixing well.
- Spread dough in a 20 cm square pan. Bake at 160°C for 20 minutes or until lightly brown.
- Let shortbread cool in pan and dust with icing sugar and cut into squares.

Nutty Blonde Brownies

1 (500 g) packet light brown sugar

4 eggs

2 cups scone mix

2 cups chopped pecans

- In a mixer, beat together the brown sugar, eggs and scone mix. Stir in pecans and pour into a greased 23 × 33 cm baking pan.
- Bake at 180°C for 35 minutes. Cool and cut into squares.

Peanut Butter Brownies

1 (600 g) packet brownie mix

1 cup peanut brittle chips

- Prepare brownie mix according to packet directions, stirring in peanut brittle chips.
- Spoon mixture into a greased 23 × 33 cm baking pan.
- Bake at 180°C for 35 minutes. Cool and cut into squares.

Snicker Brownies

1 rich chocolate cake mix

180 g butter, melted

$^1/_2$ cup evaporated milk

5 (60 g) Snicker candy bars, sliced in 3 mm slices

- In a large bowl combine cake mix, butter and evaporated milk. Beat on low speed until well blended.
- Add $^1/_2$ of the batter into a greased and floured 23 × 33 cm baking pan.
- Bake at 180°C for 10 minutes.
- Remove from oven and place candy bar slices evenly over the brownies. Drop remaining half of batter by spoonfuls over the candy bars; spread as evenly as possible.
- Place back in the oven and bake for 20 minutes longer. When cool cut into bars.

Walnut Bars

1 (170 g) packet biscuit base (crumbs)

$1^1/_2$ cups coarsely chopped walnuts

1 (400 g) can sweetened condensed milk

$^1/_4$ cup coconut (optional)

- Place the biscuit crumbs and walnuts in a bowl. Slowly add the condensed milk, coconut and a pinch of salt. Mixture will be very thick.
- Pack into a 23 cm square greased pan. Pack mixture down with the back of a spoon.
- Bake at 180°C for 35 minutes. When cool, cut into squares.

Apricot Bars

$1\frac{1}{4}$ cups flour

$\frac{3}{4}$ cup packed brown sugar

90 g butter

$\frac{3}{4}$ cup apricot jam

- In a mixing bowl, combine flour, brown sugar and rub in butter, mixing well.
- Spread half of this mixture into a 23 cm square baking pan. Spread the apricot jam over top of mixture. Add remaining flour mixture over top of dessert.
- Bake at 180°C for 30 minutes. Cut into squares.

Chocolate Drops

1 (375 g) packet milk choc-bits

$\frac{2}{3}$ cup chunky peanut butter

$4\frac{1}{4}$ cups Coco Pops cereal or rice bubbles

- In a double boiler, melt chocolate chips and stir in peanut butter. Stir in cereal.
- Press into a 23 × 33 cm pan. Cut into bars.

Pecan Squares

1 (750 g) packet almond brittle

1 cup cinnamon chips

1 cup chopped pecans

8 cups crispy rice bubble cereal

- Melt almond brittle and cinnamon chips in a very large saucepan or roaster on low heat, stirring constantly. When melted remove from heat and add pecans and frosted crispy rice bubble cereal.
- Mix well and stir into a 23 × 33 cm pan. Pat down with the back of a spoon. Refrigerate just until set. Cut into squares.

Chocolate-Cherry Bars

1 rich chocolate cake mix

1 (720 g) can pitted cherries, drained

2 eggs

1 cup milk choc-bits

- In a large bowl, mixing by hand combine all four ingredients, blending well.
- Pour batter into a greased and floured 23 × 33 cm baking dish.
- Bake at 180°C for 25 to 30 minutes or until skewer comes out clean. Cool and frost.

Frosting for Chocolate Cherry Bars

1 (85 g) square of dark chocolate, melted

1 (85 g) packet cream cheese, softened

½ teaspoon vanilla

1½ cups icing sugar

- In a medium bowl beat chocolate, cream cheese and vanilla until smooth. Gradually beat in icing sugar.
- Pour over chocolate cherry bars.

Corn Flake Cookies

1 (340 g) packet butterscotch morsels

¾ cup peanut butter

3½ to 4 cups corn flakes, crushed

- Melt butterscotch morsels on very low heat. Add peanut butter. When mixed thoroughly add corn flakes.
- Drop by teaspoons onto waxed paper.

Butterscotch Crunchies

1 (340 g) packet butterscotch morsels

$1^3/_4$ cups chow mein noodles

1 cup chopped pecans

- Melt butterscotch morsels in heavy pan over a very low flame, stirring gently. Stir in noodles and pecans just until blended and coated.
- Drop mixture by teaspoonful onto waxed paper. Refrigerate 30 minutes or until set.

Porcupine Clusters

$^1/_4$ cup corn syrup

1 (375 g) packet white choc-bits

2 cups chow mein noodles

$^3/_4$ cup salted peanuts

- On low heat, melt corn syrup and white choc-bits. Pour over noodles and peanuts. Mixing well.
- Drop by teaspoon onto baking paper.
- Refrigerate to harden. Store in airtight container.

Chocolate or butterscotch chips could be used instead of white chocolate morsels.

Hazel's Nutty Fudge

1 (375 g) packet white chocolate choc-bits

$^3/_4$ cup Nutella hazelnut-cocoa spread

$1^1/_2$ cups chopped hazelnuts, divided

- In a medium saucepan over low heat, melt the white chocolate chips and add the hazelnut spread.
- Cook and stir until mixture is well blended.
- Remove from heat and stir in 1 cup hazelnuts.
- Drop by teaspoon onto baking paper. Garnish with the reserved hazelnuts. Refrigerate until set.

Option: Add $^1/_4$ cup shredded or flaked coconut.

Tiger Butter

1 (500 g) white choc-bits

$^1/_2$ cup chunky peanut butter

1 cup semi-sweet choc-bits

- Line a 38 × 25 cm Swiss-roll pan with wax paper.
- Heat white chocolate in a microwave-safe bowl on high 1 to 2 minutes or until melted. Stir until smooth. Add peanut butter and microwave on high until melted. Stir again until smooth. Spread mixture evenly into prepared pan.
- In another microwave-safe bowl melt choc-bits on high until melted. Pour chocolate over peanut butter mixture and swirl through with a knife until you get desired effect. Refrigerate several hours until firm. Break into pieces.

Surprise Chocolates

1 kg white or milk chocolate

2 cups roasted peanuts

2 cups small pretzel sticks, broken

- Melt chocolate in a double boiler. Stir in peanuts and pretzels.
- Drop by teaspoonfuls onto baking paper. Work fast because mixture hardens quickly.
- Place in freezer for 1 hour before storing at room temperature.

Butterscotch Peanuts

1 (375 g) packet butterscotch morsels

2 cups chow mein noodles

1 cup dry roasted peanuts

- In a saucepan, heat butterscotch morsels over low heat until completely melted. Add noodles and peanuts and stir until each piece is coated.
- Drop from spoon onto baking paper. Cool. Store in airtight container.

Marshmallow Treats

60 g margarine

4 cups miniature marshmallows

½ cup chunky peanut butter

5 cups crispy rice bubbles cereal

- In a saucepan, melt margarine and add marshmallows. Stir until melted and add peanut butter. Remove from heat. Add cereal, stirring well.
- Press mixture into a 23 × 33 cm pan. Cut into squares when cool.

Honey-Nut Bars

⅓ cup margarine or butter

¼ cup cocoa

3 (100 g) packets miniature marshmallows

6 cups of Honey Nut Clusters cereal or other

- Melt margarine in a large saucepan and stir in the cocoa and marshmallows. Cook over low heat, stirring constantly until marshmallows are melted and mixture is smooth.
- Remove from heat and stir in honey nut cereal.
- Pour into an oil sprayed 18 × 28 cm pan. With a spatula smooth mixture down in pan. Cool completely and cut into bars.

Crazy Cocoa Crisps

500 g white choc-bits

$1^3/_4$ cups cocoa flavoured crispy rice cereal

2 cups dry roasted peanuts

- Place choc-bits in double boiler; heat and stir while choc-bits are melting. Stir in cereal and peanuts.
- Drop by teaspoon onto baking sheet.
- Place in refrigerator for about 30 minutes to set. Store in airtight container.

Morning Meringues

2 egg whites, beaten stiff

$^3/_4$ cup sugar

1 cup nuts

1 cup chocolate chips (choc-bits)

- Add sugar to stiffly beaten egg whites. Add in nuts and chocolate chips.
- Line a baking sheet with foil. Drop by teaspoonfuls, pressing down.
- Bake at 180°C for 10 minutes. Turn oven off. Let cookies sit in oven 8 to 10 hours.

Peanut Clusters

1 (500 g) packet white choc-bits

1 (375 g) packet milk choc-bits

5 cups salted peanuts

- In a double boiler, melt the white choc-bits and milk choc-bits.
- Stir in peanuts and drop by teaspoon onto waxed paper.
- Place in refrigerator for 30 minutes to set. Store in airtight container.

Peanutty Cocoa Puffs

$^{3}/_{4}$ cup light corn syrup

$1^{1}/_{4}$ cups sugar

$1^{1}/_{4}$ cups chunky peanut butter

$4^{1}/_{2}$ cups cocoa puff cereal

- In a large saucepan bring syrup and sugar to a rolling boil. Stir in peanut butter; mixing well. Stir in cocoa puffs.
- Drop onto waxed paper by teaspoonful.

Scotch Crunchies

$^{1}/_{2}$ cup crunchy peanut butter

1 (170 g) packet butterscotch bits

$2^{1}/_{2}$ cups frosted flakes cereal

$^{1}/_{2}$ cup peanuts

- Combine peanut butter and butterscotch bits in a large saucepan; melt over low heat. Stir until butterscotch bits are melted. Stir in cereal and peanuts.
- Drop by teaspoonfuls onto waxed paper. Refrigerate until firm. Store in airtight container.

Peanut Butter Crunchies

1 cup sugar

$^{1}/_{2}$ cup white corn syrup

2 cups peanut butter

4 cups rice bubbles cereal

- In a saucepan mix sugar and syrup and bring to a rolling boil. Remove from stove and stir in peanut butter. Add the rice bubbles, mixing well.
- Drop by the teaspoon onto waxed paper. Place in refrigerator for a few minutes to set.

Kid's Bars

1 cup each sugar and light corn syrup

$1^1/_2$ cups crunchy peanut butter

6 cups rice bubbles cereal

1 (375 g) packet chocolate chips (choc-bits)

- In a saucepan, combine sugar and corn syrup. Bring to the boil, stirring constantly. Remove from heat and stir in peanut butter and rice bubbles.
- Spread into a buttered 23 × 33 cm pan.
- In saucepan, over low heat, melt choc-bits. Spread over cereal layer. Refrigerate until set; cut into bars. Store in refrigerator.

Tasty Treat

2 cups butterscotch morsels

2 cups salted peanuts

2 cups white raisins

- Mix all ingredients together and store in an airtight container.

Brown Sugar Cookies

$^3/_4$ cup packed brown sugar

1 cup butter, softened

1 egg yolk

2 cups flour

- Cream sugar and butter until light and fluffy. Mix in egg yolk. Blend in flour. Refrigerate dough for 1 hour.
- Form dough into $2^1/_2$ cm balls, flatten and crisscross with fork on lightly greased baking sheet.
- Bake at 160°C for 10 to 12 minutes or until golden brown.

Macadamia Candy

170 g Macadamia nuts

1 (200 g) packet white choc-bits

3/4 cup coconut

- Heat a dry frying pan; toast nuts until slightly golden. (Some brands of Macadamia nuts are already toasted, so skip this step if they are.) Set aside.
- In a double boiler, melt the choc-bits.
- As soon as the choc-bits are melted, pour the Macadamia nuts and coconut in. Stir well.
- Place a piece of waxed paper on a baking sheet and pour the candy on the waxed paper; spread out. Refrigerate 30 minutes to set. Break into pieces.

Diamond Fudge

1/2 (375 g) packet semi-sweet choc-bits

1 cup creamy peanut butter

120 g margarine

1 cup icing sugar

- Cook first 3 ingredients in a saucepan over low heat, stirring constantly, just until mixture melts and is smooth. Remove from heat.
- Add icing sugar, stirring until smooth.
- Spoon into a buttered 20 cm square pan; chill until firm. Cut into squares.

Peanut Butter Fudge

340 g chunky peanut butter

375 g packet milk chocolate chips

1 (395 g) can sweetened condensed milk

1 cup chopped pecans

- In a saucepan, combine peanut butter, chocolate chips and condensed milk. Heat on low, stirring constantly until chocolate is melted.
- Add pecans, mixing well. Pour into a 23 cm square buttered dish.

Raisin Fudge

1 (375 g) packet semi-sweet choc-bits

1 cup chunky peanut butter

3 cups miniature marshmallows

$^3/_4$ cup raisins

- In a saucepan melt the choc-bits and peanut butter over medium to low heat.
- Fold in the marshmallows and raisins; stir until marshmallows have melted. Pour into a 18 × 28 cm pan.
- Chill until firm. Cut into squares. Store where it is cool.

Microwave Fudge

3 cups semi-sweet choc-bits

1 (395 g) can sweetened condensed milk

60 g margarine, cut into pieces

1 cup chopped walnuts

- Combine first 3 ingredients in a 2 litre glass bowl.
- Microwave at MEDIUM for 4 to 5 minutes, stirring at $1^1/_2$ minute intervals.
- Stir in walnuts and pour into a buttered 20 cm square dish. Chill 2 hours. Cut into squares.

Dream Candy

600 mL carton cream

3 cups sugar

1 cup light corn syrup

1 cup chopped pecans

- In a saucepan, combine the cream, sugar and corn syrup. Cook to a soft-boil stage.
- Stir and beat until candy is cool.
- Add pecans and pour into a 23 cm buttered pan.

Chocolate Toffee

1 cup sugar

240 g butter

$^1/_2$ (375 g) packet semi-sweet choc-bits

1 cup chopped pecans

- In a heavy saucepan, combine sugar and butter. Cook until candy reaches a hard-crack stage. Pour onto a greased baking sheet.
- Melt choc-bits in a double boiler and spread over toffee.
- Sprinkle with pecans; pressing pecans into the chocolate.
- Chill briefly to set chocolate. Break into pieces.

Date Loaf Candy

3 cups sugar

1 cup milk

1 (500 g) box chopped dates

1 cup chopped pecans

- Combine sugar and milk in large saucepan.
- Cook to a soft-boil stage (100°C on a candy thermometer). Stir in dates. Cook to a hard boil stage (125°C), stirring constantly.
- Remove from heat; add pecans and mix well. Stir and cool until stiff. Pour mixture onto a damp tea towel.
- Roll into a log. Let stand until set. When candy is set, remove the tea towel and slice.

Pecan-Topped Toffee

240 g butter (the real thing)

$1\frac{1}{4}$ cups packed brown sugar

6 (45 g) milk chocolate bars

$\frac{2}{3}$ cup finely chopped pecans

- In a saucepan combine the butter and sugar. Cook on medium high heat, stirring constantly until mixture reaches 150°C on candy thermometer. Pour immediately into a greased 23 cm baking pan.
- Lay chocolate bars evenly over hot candy. When the candy is soft, spread into a smooth layer.
- Sprinkle pecans over the chocolate and press lightly with the back of your spoon. Chill in refrigerator for about 1 hour.
- Invert candy onto a piece of waxed paper and break into small irregular pieces.

Yummy Pralines

120 g butter (the real thing)

1 (500 g) packet light brown sugar

1 (300 mL) carton thickened cream, unwhipped

2½ cups whole pecans

- In a heavy saucepan, combine butter, brown sugar and cream.
- Cook until temperature comes to a soft ball stage (about 20 minutes), stirring constantly. Remove from heat and set aside for about 5 minutes.
- Fold in the pecans, stirring until ingredients are glassy. (This will take several minutes of stirring.)
- With a large spoon, drop on waxed paper. Remove after pralines have cooled.

Index

B

Substitutions

Food	Amount	Substitution
Breadcrumbs, dry	1 cup	$^3/_4$ cup cracker crumbs
Broth, chicken or beef	1 cup	1 stock cube; 1 teaspoon granules in 1 cup boiling water
Butter	1 cup (125 g)	$^7/_8$ cup vegetable oil or shortening; 1 cup margarine
Buttermilk	1 cup	1 tablespoon lemon juice or white vinegar plus milk to equal 1 cup (must stand for 5 minutes)
Cottage cheese	1 cup	1 cup ricotta
Cornstarch	1 tablespoon	2 tablespoons flour
Cream, whipping	1 cup	125 g frozen whipped topping
Flour	1 cup sifted plain 1 cup sifted self-rising	1 cup minus 2 tablespoons unsifted plain 1 cup sifted plain flour plus $1^1/_2$ teaspoons baking powder plus $^1/_8$ teaspoon salt
Garlic	1 small clove	$^1/_8$ teaspoon garlic powder
Herbs	1 tablespoon fresh	1 teaspoon dried
Honey	1 cup	$1^1/_4$ cups granulated sugar plus $^1/_3$ cup liquid in recipe
Ketchup	$^1/_2$ cup	$^1/_2$ cup tomato sauce plus 2 tablespoons sugar plus 1 tablespoon vinegar
Lemon juice	1 teaspoon	$^1/_2$ teaspoon vinegar
Mushrooms	250 g fresh	1 (185 g) can, drained
Mustard	1 tablespoon prepared	1 teaspoon dried
Onions	1 small	1 tablespoon instant minced; $^1/_2$ tablespoon onion powder
Sour cream	1 cup	1 cup plain yoghurt; $^3/_4$ cup buttermilk; 1 tablespoon lemon juice plus enough evaporated milk to equal 1 cup
Sugar	1 cup light brown 1 cup granualted	$^1/_2$ packed brown sugar plus $^1/_2$ cup granulated sugar $1^3/_4$ cups confectioners sugar; 1 cup packed brown sugar; 1 cup superfine sugar
Tomato juice	1 cup	$^1/_2$ cup tomato sauce plus $^1/_2$ cup water
Tomato sauce	1 cup	$^1/_2$ cup tomato paste plus $^1/_2$ cup water
Yoghurt	1 cup	1 cup buttermilk; 1 cup milk plus 1 tablespoon lemon juice

Measurements

1 teaspoon ...... 5 mL

1 tablespoon ..... 20 mL

½ cup ...... 125 mL

1 cup ..... 250 mL

4 cups ...... 1 litre

Dry

metric (grams)	imperial (ounces)
30 g	1 oz
60 g	2 oz
90 g	3 oz
100 g	3½ oz
125 g	4 oz
150 g	5 oz
185 g	6 oz
200 g	7 oz
250 g	8 oz
280 g	9 oz
315 g	10 oz
330 g	11 oz
370 g	12 oz
400 g	13 oz
440 g	14 oz
470 g	15 oz
500 g	16 oz (1 lb)
750 g	24 oz (1½ lb)
1000 g (1 kg)	32 oz (2 lb)

Liquids

metric (millilitres)	imperial (fluid ounces)
30 mL	1 fl oz
60 mL	2 fl oz
90 mL	3 fl oz
100 mL	$3^1/_2$ fl oz
125 mL	4 fl oz
150 mL	5 fl oz
190 mL	6 fl oz
250 mL	8 fl oz
300 mL	10 fl oz
500 mL	16 fl oz
600 mL	20 fl oz (1 pint)*
1000 mL (1 litre)	32 fl oz

* Note: an American pint is 16 fl oz.

cooking temperatures	°C (celsius)	°F (fahrenheit)	gas mark
very slow	120	250	1/2
slow	150	300	2
moderately slow	160	315	2–3
moderate	180	350	4
moderate hot	190	375	5
	200	400	6
hot	220	425	7
very hot	230	450	8
	240	475	9
	250	500	10

Pan Sizes

Pan Sizes	Approximate Volume
Muffin Pans	
$1\frac{3}{4}$ x $\frac{3}{4}$ mini	$\frac{1}{8}$ cup (2 tablespoons)
$2\frac{3}{4}$ x $1\frac{1}{8}$	$\frac{1}{4}$ cup
$2\frac{3}{4}$ x $1\frac{3}{8}$	scant $\frac{1}{2}$ cup
3 x $1\frac{1}{4}$ cup jumbo	$\frac{5}{8}$ cup
Loaf Pans	
$5\frac{1}{2}$ x 3 x $2\frac{1}{2}$	2 cups
6 x $4\frac{1}{2}$ x 3	3 cups
8 x 4 x $2\frac{1}{4}$	4 cups
$8\frac{1}{2}$ x $4\frac{1}{2}$ x 3	5 cups
9 x 5 x 3	8 cups
Pie Pans	
7 x $1\frac{1}{4}$	2 cups
8 x $1\frac{1}{4}$	3 cups
8 x $1\frac{1}{2}$	4 cups
9 x $1\frac{1}{4}$	4 cups
9 x $1\frac{1}{2}$	5 cups
10 x 2	6 cups

Pan Sizes	Approximate Volume
Cake Pans	
5 x 2 round	$2\frac{2}{3}$ cups
6 x 2 round	$3\frac{3}{4}$ cups
8 x $1\frac{1}{2}$ round	4 cups
7 x 2 round	$5\frac{1}{4}$ cups
8 x 2 round	6 cups
9 x $1\frac{1}{2}$ round	6 cups
9 x 2 round	8 cups
9 x 3 bundt (ring)	9 cups
10 x $3\frac{1}{2}$ bundt (ring)	12 cups
$9\frac{1}{2}$ x $2\frac{1}{2}$ springform	10 cups
10 x $2\frac{1}{2}$ springform	12 cups
8 x 3 tube	9 cups
9 x 4 tube	11 cups
10 x 4 tube	16 cups
Casseroles	
8 x 8 x 12 square	8 cups
11 x 7 x 2 rectangular	8 cups
9 x 9 x 2 square	10 cups
13 x 9 x 2 rectangular	15 cups

Tear-out Grocery List

FRESH PRODUCE

___ Apples
___ Avocados
___ Bananas
___ Beans
___ Bell Peppers
___ Broccoli
___ Cabbage
___ Carrots
___ Cauliflower
___ Celery
___ Corn
___ Cucumbers
___ Garlic
___ Grapefruit
___ Grapes
___ Lemons
___ Lettuce
___ Lime
___ Melons
___ Mushrooms
___ Onions
___ Oranges
___ Peaches
___ Pears
___ Peppers
___ Potatoes
___ Strawberries
___ Spinach
___ Squash
___ Tomatoes
___ Zucchini
___ ____________
___ ____________

FRESH BAKERY

___ Bagels
___ Bread
___ Cake
___ Cookies
___ Croissants
___ Donuts
___ French Bread
___ Muffins
___ Pastries
___ Pies
___ Rolls
___ ____________
___ ____________

DAIRY

___ Biscuits
___ Butter
___ Cheese
___ Cheese
___ Cottage Cheese
___ Cream Cheese
___ Cream
___ Creamer
___ Eggs
___ Juice
___ Margarine
___ Milk
___ Pudding
___ Sour Cream
___ Yogurt
___ ____________
___ ____________

DELI

___ Chicken
___ Main Dish
___ Prepared Salad
___ Sandwich Meat
___ Side Dishes
___ ____________
___ ____________

FROZEN FOODS

___ Breakfast
___ Dinners
___ Ice
___ ce Cream
___ Juice
___ Pastries
___ Pies
___ Pizza
___ Potatoes
___ Vegetables
___ Whipped Cream
___ ____________
___ ____________

OTHER

___ ____________
___ ____________
___ ____________
___ ____________
___ ____________
___ ____________
___ ____________

Tear-out Grocery List

GROCERY

- ___ Beans
- ___ Beer/Wine
- ___ Bread
- ___ Canned Vegetables
- ___ ____________
- ___ ____________
- ___ Cereal
- ___ Chips/Snacks
- ___ Coffee
- ___ Cookies
- ___ Crackers
- ___ Flour
- ___ Honey
- ___ Jelly
- ___ Juice
- ___ Ketchup
- ___ Kool-Aid
- ___ Mayonnaise
- ___ Mixes
- ___ ____________
- ___ ____________
- ___ Mustard
- ___ Nuts/Seeds
- ___ Oil
- ___ Pasta
- ___ Peanut Butter
- ___ Pickles/Olives
- ___ Popcorn
- ___ Rice
- ___ Salad Dressing
- ___ Salt
- ___ Seasonings
- ___ ____________
- ___ ____________
- ___ Sauce
- ___ Sodas
- ___ Soups
- ___ Spices
- ___ ____________
- ___ ____________
- ___ ____________
- ___ Sugar
- ___ Syrup
- ___ Tea
- ___ Tortillas
- ___ Water
- ___ ____________
- ___ ____________
- ___ ____________
- ___ ____________
- ___ ____________

MEAT

- ___ Bacon
- ___ Chicken
- ___ Ground Beef
- ___ Ham
- ___ Hot Dogs
- ___ Pork
- ___ Roast
- ___ Sandwich Meat
- ___ Sausage
- ___ Steak
- ___ Turkey
- ___ ____________
- ___ ____________
- ___ ____________

GENERAL MERCHANDISE

- ___ Automotive
- ___ Baby Items
- ___ ____________
- ___ ____________
- ___ ____________
- ___ Bath Soap
- ___ Bath Tissue
- ___ Deodorant
- ___ Detergent
- ___ Dish Soap
- ___ Facial Tissue
- ___ Feminine Products
- ___ Aluminum Foil
- ___ Greeting Cards
- ___ Hardware
- ___ Insecticides
- ___ Light Bulbs
- ___ Lotion
- ___ Medicine
- ___ Napkins
- ___ Paper Plates
- ___ Paper Towels
- ___ Pet Supplies
- ___ Prescriptions
- ___ Shampoo
- ___ Toothpaste
- ___ Vitamins
- ___ ____________
- ___ ____________
- ___ ____________
- ___ ____________
- ___ ____________
- ___ ____________

Tear-out Grocery List

FRESH PRODUCE

___ Apples
___ Avocados
___ Bananas
___ Beans
___ Bell Peppers
___ Broccoli
___ Cabbage
___ Carrots
___ Cauliflower
___ Celery
___ Corn
___ Cucumbers
___ Garlic
___ Grapefruit
___ Grapes
___ Lemons
___ Lettuce
___ Lime
___ Melons
___ Mushrooms
___ Onions
___ Oranges
___ Peaches
___ Pears
___ Peppers
___ Potatoes
___ Strawberries
___ Spinach
___ Squash
___ Tomatoes
___ Zucchini
___ ______________
___ ______________

FRESH BAKERY

___ Bagels
___ Bread
___ Cake
___ Cookies
___ Croissants
___ Donuts
___ French Bread
___ Muffins
___ Pastries
___ Pies
___ Rolls
___ ______________
___ ______________

DAIRY

___ Biscuits
___ Butter
___ Cheese
___ Cheese
___ Cottage Cheese
___ Cream Cheese
___ Cream
___ Creamer
___ Eggs
___ Juice
___ Margarine
___ Milk
___ Pudding
___ Sour Cream
___ Yogurt
___ ______________
___ ______________

DELI

___ Chicken
___ Main Dish
___ Prepared Salad
___ Sandwich Meat
___ Side Dishes
___ ______________
___ ______________

FROZEN FOODS

___ Breakfast
___ Dinners
___ Ice
___ ce Cream
___ Juice
___ Pastries
___ Pies
___ Pizza
___ Potatoes
___ Vegetables
___ Whipped Cream
___ ______________
___ ______________

OTHER

___ ______________
___ ______________
___ ______________
___ ______________
___ ______________
___ ______________
___ ______________

Tear-out Grocery List

GROCERY

___ Beans
___ Beer/Wine
___ Bread
___ Canned Vegetables
___ ______________
___ ______________
___ Cereal
___ Chips/Snacks
___ Coffee
___ Cookies
___ Crackers
___ Flour
___ Honey
___ Jelly
___ Juice
___ Ketchup
___ Kool-Aid
___ Mayonnaise
___ Mixes
___ ______________
___ ______________
___ Mustard
___ Nuts/Seeds
___ Oil
___ Pasta
___ Peanut Butter
___ Pickles/Olives
___ Popcorn
___ Rice
___ Salad Dressing
___ Salt
___ Seasonings
___ ______________
___ ______________
___ Sauce
___ Sodas
___ Soups
___ Spices
___ ______________
___ ______________
___ ______________
___ Sugar
___ Syrup
___ Tea
___ Tortillas
___ Water
___ ______________
___ ______________
___ ______________
___ ______________
___ ______________

MEAT

___ Bacon
___ Chicken
___ Ground Beef
___ Ham
___ Hot Dogs
___ Pork
___ Roast
___ Sandwich Meat
___ Sausage
___ Steak
___ Turkey
___ ______________
___ ______________
___ ______________

GENERAL MERCHANDISE

___ Automotive
___ Baby Items
___ ______________
___ ______________
___ ______________
___ Bath Soap
___ Bath Tissue
___ Deodorant
___ Detergent
___ Dish Soap
___ Facial Tissue
___ Feminine Products
___ Aluminum Foil
___ Greeting Cards
___ Hardware
___ Insecticides
___ Light Bulbs
___ Lotion
___ Medicine
___ Napkins
___ Paper Plates
___ Paper Towels
___ Pet Supplies
___ Prescriptions
___ Shampoo
___ Toothpaste
___ Vitamins
___ ______________
___ ______________
___ ______________
___ ______________
___ ______________
___ ______________

Tear-out Grocery List

FRESH PRODUCE

___ Apples
___ Avocados
___ Bananas
___ Beans
___ Bell Peppers
___ Broccoli
___ Cabbage
___ Carrots
___ Cauliflower
___ Celery
___ Corn
___ Cucumbers
___ Garlic
___ Grapefruit
___ Grapes
___ Lemons
___ Lettuce
___ Lime
___ Melons
___ Mushrooms
___ Onions
___ Oranges
___ Peaches
___ Pears
___ Peppers
___ Potatoes
___ Strawberries
___ Spinach
___ Squash
___ Tomatoes
___ Zucchini
___ ____________
___ ____________

FRESH BAKERY

___ Bagels
___ Bread
___ Cake
___ Cookies
___ Croissants
___ Donuts
___ French Bread
___ Muffins
___ Pastries
___ Pies
___ Rolls
___ ____________
___ ____________

DAIRY

___ Biscuits
___ Butter
___ Cheese
___ Cheese
___ Cottage Cheese
___ Cream Cheese
___ Cream
___ Creamer
___ Eggs
___ Juice
___ Margarine
___ Milk
___ Pudding
___ Sour Cream
___ Yogurt
___ ____________
___ ____________

DELI

___ Chicken
___ Main Dish
___ Prepared Salad
___ Sandwich Meat
___ Side Dishes
___ ____________
___ ____________

FROZEN FOODS

___ Breakfast
___ Dinners
___ Ice
___ ce Cream
___ Juice
___ Pastries
___ Pies
___ Pizza
___ Potatoes
___ Vegetables
___ Whipped Cream
___ ____________
___ ____________

OTHER

___ ____________
___ ____________
___ ____________
___ ____________
___ ____________
___ ____________
___ ____________

Tear-out Grocery List

GROCERY
___ Beans
___ Beer/Wine
___ Bread
___ Canned Vegetables
___ ____________
___ ____________
___ Cereal
___ Chips/Snacks
___ Coffee
___ Cookies
___ Crackers
___ Flour
___ Honey
___ Jelly
___ Juice
___ Ketchup
___ Kool-Aid
___ Mayonnaise
___ Mixes
___ ____________
___ ____________
___ Mustard
___ Nuts/Seeds
___ Oil
___ Pasta
___ Peanut Butter
___ Pickles/Olives
___ Popcorn
___ Rice
___ Salad Dressing
___ Salt
___ Seasonings
___ ____________
___ ____________
___ Sauce
___ Sodas
___ Soups
___ Spices
___ ____________
___ ____________
___ ____________
___ Sugar
___ Syrup
___ Tea
___ Tortillas
___ Water
___ ____________
___ ____________
___ ____________
___ ____________
___ ____________

MEAT
___ Bacon
___ Chicken
___ Ground Beef
___ Ham
___ Hot Dogs
___ Pork
___ Roast
___ Sandwich Meat
___ Sausage
___ Steak
___ Turkey
___ ____________
___ ____________
___ ____________

GENERAL MERCHANDISE
___ Automotive
___ Baby Items
___ ____________
___ ____________
___ ____________
___ Bath Soap
___ Bath Tissue
___ Deodorant
___ Detergent
___ Dish Soap
___ Facial Tissue
___ Feminine Products
___ Aluminum Foil
___ Greeting Cards
___ Hardware
___ Insecticides
___ Light Bulbs
___ Lotion
___ Medicine
___ Napkins
___ Paper Plates
___ Paper Towels
___ Pet Supplies
___ Prescriptions
___ Shampoo
___ Toothpaste
___ Vitamins
___ ____________
___ ____________
___ ____________
___ ____________
___ ____________
___ ____________

Tear-out Grocery List

FRESH PRODUCE

___ Apples
___ Avocados
___ Bananas
___ Beans
___ Bell Peppers
___ Broccoli
___ Cabbage
___ Carrots
___ Cauliflower
___ Celery
___ Corn
___ Cucumbers
___ Garlic
___ Grapefruit
___ Grapes
___ Lemons
___ Lettuce
___ Lime
___ Melons
___ Mushrooms
___ Onions
___ Oranges
___ Peaches
___ Pears
___ Peppers
___ Potatoes
___ Strawberries
___ Spinach
___ Squash
___ Tomatoes
___ Zucchini
___ ____________
___ ____________

FRESH BAKERY

___ Bagels
___ Bread
___ Cake
___ Cookies
___ Croissants
___ Donuts
___ French Bread
___ Muffins
___ Pastries
___ Pies
___ Rolls
___ ____________
___ ____________

DAIRY

___ Biscuits
___ Butter
___ Cheese
___ Cheese
___ Cottage Cheese
___ Cream Cheese
___ Cream
___ Creamer
___ Eggs
___ Juice
___ Margarine
___ Milk
___ Pudding
___ Sour Cream
___ Yogurt
___ ____________
___ ____________

DELI

___ Chicken
___ Main Dish
___ Prepared Salad
___ Sandwich Meat
___ Side Dishes
___ ____________
___ ____________

FROZEN FOODS

___ Breakfast
___ Dinners
___ Ice
___ ce Cream
___ Juice
___ Pastries
___ Pies
___ Pizza
___ Potatoes
___ Vegetables
___ Whipped Cream
___ ____________
___ ____________

OTHER

___ ____________
___ ____________
___ ____________
___ ____________
___ ____________
___ ____________
___ ____________

Tear-out Grocery List

GROCERY

___ Beans
___ Beer/Wine
___ Bread
___ Canned Vegetables
___ ____________
___ ____________
___ Cereal
___ Chips/Snacks
___ Coffee
___ Cookies
___ Crackers
___ Flour
___ Honey
___ Jelly
___ Juice
___ Ketchup
___ Kool-Aid
___ Mayonnaise
___ Mixes
___ ____________
___ ____________
___ Mustard
___ Nuts/Seeds
___ Oil
___ Pasta
___ Peanut Butter
___ Pickles/Olives
___ Popcorn
___ Rice
___ Salad Dressing
___ Salt
___ Seasonings
___ ____________
___ ____________
___ Sauce
___ Sodas
___ Soups
___ Spices
___ ____________
___ ____________
___ ____________
___ Sugar
___ Syrup
___ Tea
___ Tortillas
___ Water
___ ____________
___ ____________
___ ____________
___ ____________
___ ____________

MEAT

___ Bacon
___ Chicken
___ Ground Beef
___ Ham
___ Hot Dogs
___ Pork
___ Roast
___ Sandwich Meat
___ Sausage
___ Steak
___ Turkey
___ ____________
___ ____________
___ ____________

GENERAL MERCHANDISE

___ Automotive
___ Baby Items
___ ____________
___ ____________
___ ____________
___ Bath Soap
___ Bath Tissue
___ Deodorant
___ Detergent
___ Dish Soap
___ Facial Tissue
___ Feminine Products
___ Aluminum Foil
___ Greeting Cards
___ Hardware
___ Insecticides
___ Light Bulbs
___ Lotion
___ Medicine
___ Napkins
___ Paper Plates
___ Paper Towels
___ Pet Supplies
___ Prescriptions
___ Shampoo
___ Toothpaste
___ Vitamins
___ ____________
___ ____________
___ ____________
___ ____________
___ ____________
___ ____________

Tear-out Grocery List

FRESH PRODUCE

___ Apples
___ Avocados
___ Bananas
___ Beans
___ Bell Peppers
___ Broccoli
___ Cabbage
___ Carrots
___ Cauliflower
___ Celery
___ Corn
___ Cucumbers
___ Garlic
___ Grapefruit
___ Grapes
___ Lemons
___ Lettuce
___ Lime
___ Melons
___ Mushrooms
___ Onions
___ Oranges
___ Peaches
___ Pears
___ Peppers
___ Potatoes
___ Strawberries
___ Spinach
___ Squash
___ Tomatoes
___ Zucchini
___ ____________
___ ____________

FRESH BAKERY

___ Bagels
___ Bread
___ Cake
___ Cookies
___ Croissants
___ Donuts
___ French Bread
___ Muffins
___ Pastries
___ Pies
___ Rolls
___ ____________
___ ____________

DAIRY

___ Biscuits
___ Butter
___ Cheese
___ Cheese
___ Cottage Cheese
___ Cream Cheese
___ Cream
___ Creamer
___ Eggs
___ Juice
___ Margarine
___ Milk
___ Pudding
___ Sour Cream
___ Yogurt
___ ____________
___ ____________

DELI

___ Chicken
___ Main Dish
___ Prepared Salad
___ Sandwich Meat
___ Side Dishes
___ ____________
___ ____________

FROZEN FOODS

___ Breakfast
___ Dinners
___ Ice
___ ce Cream
___ Juice
___ Pastries
___ Pies
___ Pizza
___ Potatoes
___ Vegetables
___ Whipped Cream
___ ____________
___ ____________

OTHER

___ ____________
___ ____________
___ ____________
___ ____________
___ ____________
___ ____________
___ ____________

Tear-out Grocery List

GROCERY

- ___ Beans
- ___ Beer/Wine
- ___ Bread
- ___ Canned Vegetables
- ___ ______________
- ___ ______________
- ___ Cereal
- ___ Chips/Snacks
- ___ Coffee
- ___ Cookies
- ___ Crackers
- ___ Flour
- ___ Honey
- ___ Jelly
- ___ Juice
- ___ Ketchup
- ___ Kool-Aid
- ___ Mayonnaise
- ___ Mixes
- ___ ______________
- ___ ______________
- ___ Mustard
- ___ Nuts/Seeds
- ___ Oil
- ___ Pasta
- ___ Peanut Butter
- ___ Pickles/Olives
- ___ Popcorn
- ___ Rice
- ___ Salad Dressing
- ___ Salt
- ___ Seasonings
- ___ ______________
- ___ ______________
- ___ Sauce
- ___ Sodas
- ___ Soups
- ___ Spices
- ___ ______________
- ___ ______________
- ___ ______________
- ___ Sugar
- ___ Syrup
- ___ Tea
- ___ Tortillas
- ___ Water
- ___ ______________
- ___ ______________
- ___ ______________
- ___ ______________
- ___ ______________

MEAT

- ___ Bacon
- ___ Chicken
- ___ Ground Beef
- ___ Ham
- ___ Hot Dogs
- ___ Pork
- ___ Roast
- ___ Sandwich Meat
- ___ Sausage
- ___ Steak
- ___ Turkey
- ___ ______________
- ___ ______________
- ___ ______________

GENERAL MERCHANDISE

- ___ Automotive
- ___ Baby Items
- ___ ______________
- ___ ______________
- ___ ______________
- ___ Bath Soap
- ___ Bath Tissue
- ___ Deodorant
- ___ Detergent
- ___ Dish Soap
- ___ Facial Tissue
- ___ Feminine Products
- ___ Aluminum Foil
- ___ Greeting Cards
- ___ Hardware
- ___ Insecticides
- ___ Light Bulbs
- ___ Lotion
- ___ Medicine
- ___ Napkins
- ___ Paper Plates
- ___ Paper Towels
- ___ Pet Supplies
- ___ Prescriptions
- ___ Shampoo
- ___ Toothpaste
- ___ Vitamins
- ___ ______________
- ___ ______________
- ___ ______________
- ___ ______________
- ___ ______________
- ___ ______________

Tear-out Grocery List

FRESH PRODUCE

___ Apples
___ Avocados
___ Bananas
___ Beans
___ Bell Peppers
___ Broccoli
___ Cabbage
___ Carrots
___ Cauliflower
___ Celery
___ Corn
___ Cucumbers
___ Garlic
___ Grapefruit
___ Grapes
___ Lemons
___ Lettuce
___ Lime
___ Melons
___ Mushrooms
___ Onions
___ Oranges
___ Peaches
___ Pears
___ Peppers
___ Potatoes
___ Strawberries
___ Spinach
___ Squash
___ Tomatoes
___ Zucchini
___ ______________
___ ______________

FRESH BAKERY

___ Bagels
___ Bread
___ Cake
___ Cookies
___ Croissants
___ Donuts
___ French Bread
___ Muffins
___ Pastries
___ Pies
___ Rolls
___ ______________
___ ______________

DAIRY

___ Biscuits
___ Butter
___ Cheese
___ Cheese
___ Cottage Cheese
___ Cream Cheese
___ Cream
___ Creamer
___ Eggs
___ Juice
___ Margarine
___ Milk
___ Pudding
___ Sour Cream
___ Yogurt
___ ______________
___ ______________

DELI

___ Chicken
___ Main Dish
___ Prepared Salad
___ Sandwich Meat
___ Side Dishes
___ ______________
___ ______________

FROZEN FOODS

___ Breakfast
___ Dinners
___ Ice
___ ce Cream
___ Juice
___ Pastries
___ Pies
___ Pizza
___ Potatoes
___ Vegetables
___ Whipped Cream
___ ______________
___ ______________

OTHER

___ ______________
___ ______________
___ ______________
___ ______________
___ ______________
___ ______________
___ ______________

Tear-out Grocery List

GROCERY

___ Beans
___ Beer/Wine
___ Bread
___ Canned Vegetables
___ ____________
___ ____________
___ Cereal
___ Chips/Snacks
___ Coffee
___ Cookies
___ Crackers
___ Flour
___ Honey
___ Jelly
___ Juice
___ Ketchup
___ Kool-Aid
___ Mayonnaise
___ Mixes
___ ____________
___ ____________
___ Mustard
___ Nuts/Seeds
___ Oil
___ Pasta
___ Peanut Butter
___ Pickles/Olives
___ Popcorn
___ Rice
___ Salad Dressing
___ Salt
___ Seasonings
___ ____________
___ ____________
___ Sauce
___ Sodas
___ Soups
___ Spices
___ ____________
___ ____________
___ ____________
___ Sugar
___ Syrup
___ Tea
___ Tortillas
___ Water
___ ____________
___ ____________
___ ____________
___ ____________
___ ____________

MEAT

___ Bacon
___ Chicken
___ Ground Beef
___ Ham
___ Hot Dogs
___ Pork
___ Roast
___ Sandwich Meat
___ Sausage
___ Steak
___ Turkey
___ ____________
___ ____________
___ ____________

GENERAL MERCHANDISE

___ Automotive
___ Baby Items
___ ____________
___ ____________
___ ____________
___ Bath Soap
___ Bath Tissue
___ Deodorant
___ Detergent
___ Dish Soap
___ Facial Tissue
___ Feminine Products
___ Aluminum Foil
___ Greeting Cards
___ Hardware
___ Insecticides
___ Light Bulbs
___ Lotion
___ Medicine
___ Napkins
___ Paper Plates
___ Paper Towels
___ Pet Supplies
___ Prescriptions
___ Shampoo
___ Toothpaste
___ Vitamins
___ ____________
___ ____________
___ ____________
___ ____________
___ ____________
___ ____________

Tear-out Grocery List

FRESH PRODUCE

___ Apples
___ Avocados
___ Bananas
___ Beans
___ Bell Peppers
___ Broccoli
___ Cabbage
___ Carrots
___ Cauliflower
___ Celery
___ Corn
___ Cucumbers
___ Garlic
___ Grapefruit
___ Grapes
___ Lemons
___ Lettuce
___ Lime
___ Melons
___ Mushrooms
___ Onions
___ Oranges
___ Peaches
___ Pears
___ Peppers
___ Potatoes
___ Strawberries
___ Spinach
___ Squash
___ Tomatoes
___ Zucchini
___ ______________
___ ______________

FRESH BAKERY

___ Bagels
___ Bread
___ Cake
___ Cookies
___ Croissants
___ Donuts
___ French Bread
___ Muffins
___ Pastries
___ Pies
___ Rolls
___ ______________
___ ______________

DAIRY

___ Biscuits
___ Butter
___ Cheese
___ Cheese
___ Cottage Cheese
___ Cream Cheese
___ Cream
___ Creamer
___ Eggs
___ Juice
___ Margarine
___ Milk
___ Pudding
___ Sour Cream
___ Yogurt
___ ______________
___ ______________

DELI

___ Chicken
___ Main Dish
___ Prepared Salad
___ Sandwich Meat
___ Side Dishes
___ ______________
___ ______________

FROZEN FOODS

___ Breakfast
___ Dinners
___ Ice
___ ce Cream
___ Juice
___ Pastries
___ Pies
___ Pizza
___ Potatoes
___ Vegetables
___ Whipped Cream
___ ______________
___ ______________

OTHER

___ ______________
___ ______________
___ ______________
___ ______________
___ ______________
___ ______________
___ ______________

Tear-out Grocery List

GROCERY

- ___ Beans
- ___ Beer/Wine
- ___ Bread
- ___ Canned Vegetables
- ___ ______________
- ___ ______________
- ___ Cereal
- ___ Chips/Snacks
- ___ Coffee
- ___ Cookies
- ___ Crackers
- ___ Flour
- ___ Honey
- ___ Jelly
- ___ Juice
- ___ Ketchup
- ___ Kool-Aid
- ___ Mayonnaise
- ___ Mixes
- ___ ______________
- ___ ______________
- ___ Mustard
- ___ Nuts/Seeds
- ___ Oil
- ___ Pasta
- ___ Peanut Butter
- ___ Pickles/Olives
- ___ Popcorn
- ___ Rice
- ___ Salad Dressing
- ___ Salt
- ___ Seasonings
- ___ ______________
- ___ ______________
- ___ Sauce
- ___ Sodas
- ___ Soups
- ___ Spices
- ___ ______________
- ___ ______________
- ___ ______________
- ___ Sugar
- ___ Syrup
- ___ Tea
- ___ Tortillas
- ___ Water
- ___ ______________
- ___ ______________
- ___ ______________
- ___ ______________
- ___ ______________

MEAT

- ___ Bacon
- ___ Chicken
- ___ Ground Beef
- ___ Ham
- ___ Hot Dogs
- ___ Pork
- ___ Roast
- ___ Sandwich Meat
- ___ Sausage
- ___ Steak
- ___ Turkey
- ___ ______________
- ___ ______________
- ___ ______________

GENERAL MERCHANDISE

- ___ Automotive
- ___ Baby Items
- ___ ______________
- ___ ______________
- ___ ______________
- ___ Bath Soap
- ___ Bath Tissue
- ___ Deodorant
- ___ Detergent
- ___ Dish Soap
- ___ Facial Tissue
- ___ Feminine Products
- ___ Aluminum Foil
- ___ Greeting Cards
- ___ Hardware
- ___ Insecticides
- ___ Light Bulbs
- ___ Lotion
- ___ Medicine
- ___ Napkins
- ___ Paper Plates
- ___ Paper Towels
- ___ Pet Supplies
- ___ Prescriptions
- ___ Shampoo
- ___ Toothpaste
- ___ Vitamins
- ___ ______________
- ___ ______________
- ___ ______________
- ___ ______________
- ___ ______________
- ___ ______________

Tear-out Grocery List

FRESH PRODUCE

___ Apples
___ Avocados
___ Bananas
___ Beans
___ Bell Peppers
___ Broccoli
___ Cabbage
___ Carrots
___ Cauliflower
___ Celery
___ Corn
___ Cucumbers
___ Garlic
___ Grapefruit
___ Grapes
___ Lemons
___ Lettuce
___ Lime
___ Melons
___ Mushrooms
___ Onions
___ Oranges
___ Peaches
___ Pears
___ Peppers
___ Potatoes
___ Strawberries
___ Spinach
___ Squash
___ Tomatoes
___ Zucchini
___ ______________
___ ______________

FRESH BAKERY

___ Bagels
___ Bread
___ Cake
___ Cookies
___ Croissants
___ Donuts
___ French Bread
___ Muffins
___ Pastries
___ Pies
___ Rolls
___ ______________
___ ______________

DAIRY

___ Biscuits
___ Butter
___ Cheese
___ Cheese
___ Cottage Cheese
___ Cream Cheese
___ Cream
___ Creamer
___ Eggs
___ Juice
___ Margarine
___ Milk
___ Pudding
___ Sour Cream
___ Yogurt
___ ______________
___ ______________

DELI

___ Chicken
___ Main Dish
___ Prepared Salad
___ Sandwich Meat
___ Side Dishes
___ ______________
___ ______________

FROZEN FOODS

___ Breakfast
___ Dinners
___ Ice
___ ce Cream
___ Juice
___ Pastries
___ Pies
___ Pizza
___ Potatoes
___ Vegetables
___ Whipped Cream
___ ______________
___ ______________

OTHER

___ ______________
___ ______________
___ ______________
___ ______________
___ ______________
___ ______________
___ ______________

Tear-out Grocery List

GROCERY

___ Beans
___ Beer/Wine
___ Bread
___ Canned Vegetables
___ ____________
___ ____________
___ Cereal
___ Chips/Snacks
___ Coffee
___ Cookies
___ Crackers
___ Flour
___ Honey
___ Jelly
___ Juice
___ Ketchup
___ Kool-Aid
___ Mayonnaise
___ Mixes
___ ____________
___ ____________
___ Mustard
___ Nuts/Seeds
___ Oil
___ Pasta
___ Peanut Butter
___ Pickles/Olives
___ Popcorn
___ Rice
___ Salad Dressing
___ Salt
___ Seasonings
___ ____________
___ ____________
___ Sauce
___ Sodas
___ Soups
___ Spices
___ ____________
___ ____________
___ ____________
___ Sugar
___ Syrup
___ Tea
___ Tortillas
___ Water
___ ____________
___ ____________
___ ____________
___ ____________
___ ____________

MEAT

___ Bacon
___ Chicken
___ Ground Beef
___ Ham
___ Hot Dogs
___ Pork
___ Roast
___ Sandwich Meat
___ Sausage
___ Steak
___ Turkey
___ ____________
___ ____________
___ ____________

GENERAL MERCHANDISE

___ Automotive
___ Baby Items
___ ____________
___ ____________
___ ____________
___ Bath Soap
___ Bath Tissue
___ Deodorant
___ Detergent
___ Dish Soap
___ Facial Tissue
___ Feminine Products
___ Aluminum Foil
___ Greeting Cards
___ Hardware
___ Insecticides
___ Light Bulbs
___ Lotion
___ Medicine
___ Napkins
___ Paper Plates
___ Paper Towels
___ Pet Supplies
___ Prescriptions
___ Shampoo
___ Toothpaste
___ Vitamins
___ ____________
___ ____________
___ ____________
___ ____________
___ ____________
___ ____________